W9-AVS-823

Stahl's Illustrated

Antipsychotics:

Treating Psychosis, Mania, and Depression

Stephen M. Stahl
University of California at San Diego

Laurence Mignon
Neuroscience Education Institute, CA

Nancy Muntner
Illustrations

CAMBRIDGE
UNIVERSITY PRESS

PREFACE

These books are designed to be fun. All concepts are illustrated by full-color images. The text can be used as a supplement to figures, images, and tables. The visual learner will find that this book makes psychopharmacology concepts easy to master, while the non-visual learner may enjoy a shortened text version of complex psychopharmacology concepts. Each chapter builds upon previous chapters, synthesizing information from basic biology and diagnostics to building treatment plans and dealing with complications and comorbidities.

Novices may want to approach this Pocketbook by first looking through all the graphics, gaining a feel for the visual vocabulary on which our psychopharmacology concepts rely. After this once-over glance, we suggest going back through the book to incorporate the images with text from figure legends. Learning from visual concepts and textual supplements should reinforce one another, providing you with solid conceptual understanding at each step along the way.

Readers more familiar with these topics should find that going back and forth between images and text provides an interaction with which to vividly conceptualize complex psychopharmacology. You may find yourself using this book frequently to refresh your psychopharmacological knowledge. You may also find yourself referring your colleagues to this desk reference.

This Pocketbook is intended as a conceptual overview of different topics; we provide you with a visual-based language to incorporate the rules of psychopharmacology at the sacrifice of discussing the exceptions to these rules. A Suggested Readings section at the end of this Pocketbook gives you a good start for more in-depth learning about particular concepts presented here.

When you come across an abbreviation or figure you don't understand, you can refer to the Abbreviation and Symbols legend in the back. After referring to these several times you will begin to develop proficiency in the visual vocabulary of psychopharmacology. Stahl's Essential Psychopharmacology, 3rd Edition, and Stahl's Essential Psychopharmacology: The Prescriber's Guide, 3rd Edition can be helpful supplementary tools for more in-depth information on particular topics in this Pocketbook. Now you can also search topics in psychopharmacology on the Neuroscience Education Institute's website (www.neiglobal.com) for lectures, courses, slides and related articles.

Whether you are a novice or an experienced psychopharmacologist, hopefully this book will lead you to think critically about the complexities involved in psychiatric disorders and their treatments.

Best wishes for your educational journey into the fascinating field of psychopharmacology!

Stephen M. Stahl

Table of Contents

Disclaimer

The information presented in this educational activity is not meant to define a standard of care, nor is it intended to dictate an exclusive course of patient management. Any procedures, medications, or other courses of diagnosis or treatment discussed or suggested in this educational activity should not be used by clinicians without full evaluation of their patients' conditions and possible contraindications or dangers in use, review of any applicable manufacturer's product information, and comparison with recommendations of other authorities. Primary references and full prescribing information should be consulted.

Participants have an implied responsibility to use the newly acquired information from this activity to enhance patient outcomes and their own professional development. The participant should use his/her clinical judgment, knowledge, experience, and diagnostic decision-making before applying any information, whether provided here or by others, for any professional use.

Neurobiology of Schizophrenia and Mood Disorders

This chapter introduces the neurobiology that is thought to underlie the symptoms of schizophrenia. The dopamine hypothesis of schizophrenia has been accepted for a long time, especially as the first antipsychotics were shown to block dopamine D2 receptors. This theory posits that dopamine is overactive in some brain areas, and underactive in other brain areas. This chapter shows that it might be more accurate to say that dopamine is neither "too high" nor "too low" but "out of tune." In addition, ideas about the involvement of glutamate and serotonin have gained momentum in the pathophysiology of schizophrenia, and this chapter aims to give an overview of how these three neurotransmitter systems may come together to induce both the positive and negative symptoms of schizophrenia.

As various antipsychotics have been used in the treatment of mood disorders, this chapter will also go through the hypothetical neurobiology of disorders, such as mania and depression. Beside dopamine and serotonin, norepinephrine is also one of the main players in mood disorders, and will therefore be discussed here.

This brief neurobiological overview of the neurotransmitter systems impacted by antipsychotics will also aid in understanding the occurrence of side effects of different antipsychotics.

Key Brain Regions and Their Hypothetical Functions: Relevance to Schizophrenia

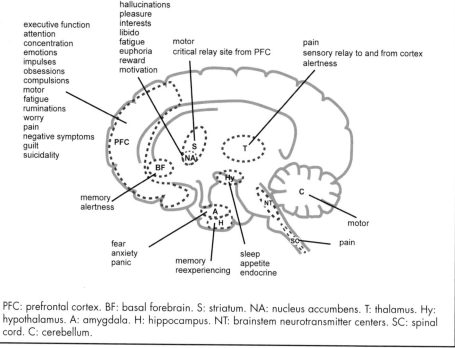

delusions
hallucinations
pleasure
interests
libido
fatigue
euphoria
reward
motivation

executive function
attention
concentration
emotions
impulses
obsessions
compulsions
motor
fatigue
ruminations
worry
pain
negative symptoms
guilt
suicidality

motor
critical relay site from PFC

pain
sensory relay to and from cortex
alertness

memory
alertness

fear
anxiety
panic

memory
reexperiencing

sleep
appetite
endocrine

motor

pain

PFC: prefrontal cortex. BF: basal forebrain. S: striatum. NA: nucleus accumbens. T: thalamus. Hy: hypothalamus. A: amygdala. H: hippocampus. NT: brainstem neurotransmitter centers. SC: spinal cord. C: cerebellum.

FIGURE 1.1. Psychiatric disorders hypothetically result from alterations in neurotransmission within different brain regions. A different set of symptoms is unveiled depending on which brain area is functionally impaired.

In schizophrenia, the neurotransmitter dopamine (DA) is theoretically dysregulated, and as a result various brain areas are overactive, underactive, or otherwise "out of tune," resulting in the generation of positive and negative symptoms.

Key DA Pathways

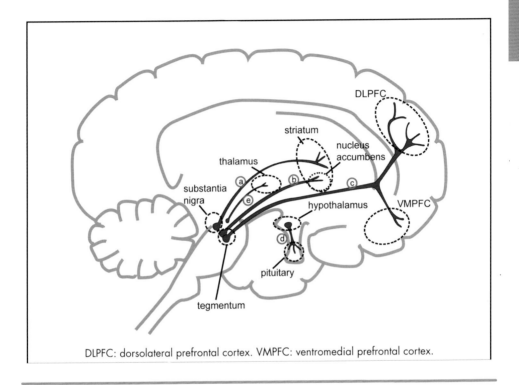

DLPFC: dorsolateral prefrontal cortex. VMPFC: ventromedial prefrontal cortex.

FIGURE 1.2. Five dopamine (DA) pathways are relevant in explaining the symptoms of schizophrenia and the therapeutic and side effects of antipsychotic drugs.

(a) The <u>nigrostriatal DA pathway</u> is part of the extrapyramidal nervous system, which controls motor function and movement.

(b) The <u>mesolimbic DA pathway</u> is part of the brain's limbic system, which regulates behaviors including pleasurable sensations, the powerful euphoria of drugs of abuse, and the delusions and hallucinations seen in psychosis.

(c) The <u>mesocortical DA pathway</u> is implicated in mediating the cognitive symptoms (dorsolateral prefrontal cortex, DLPFC) and affective symptoms (ventromedial prefrontal cortex, VMPFC) of schizophrenia.

(d) The <u>tuberoinfundibular DA pathway</u> projects from the hypothalamus to the anterior pituitary gland and controls prolactin secretion.

(e) The fifth DA pathway arises from multiple sites, including the periaqueductal gray, ventral mesencephalon, hypothalamic nuclei, and lateral parabrachial nucleus and projects to the thalamus. Its function is not well known.

The DA Hypothesis of Schizophrenia: Positive Symptoms

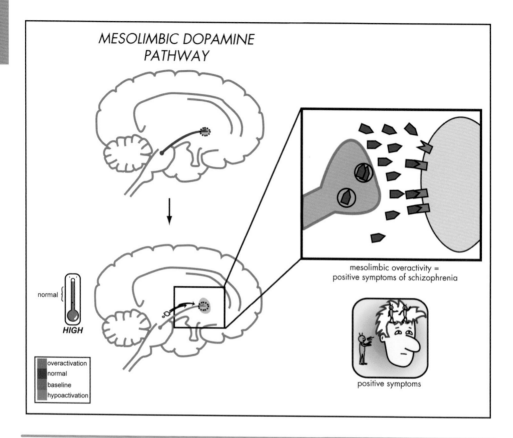

FIGURE 1.3. The mesolimbic DA pathway sends DA projections from cell bodies in the ventral tegmental area to the nucleus accumbens in the ventral striatum. This pathway hypothetically regulates emotional behaviors, pleasure, and reward and is the main candidate thought to regulate the positive symptoms of psychosis.

Specifically, it has been hypothesized that hyperactivity of this pathway accounts for the delusions and hallucinations observed in schizophrenia. This hypothesis is known both as the "DA hypothesis of schizophrenia" and perhaps more precisely as the "mesolimbic DA hyperactivity hypothesis of positive symptoms of schizophrenia."

The DA Hypothesis of Schizophrenia:
Negative, Cognitive, and Affective Symptoms

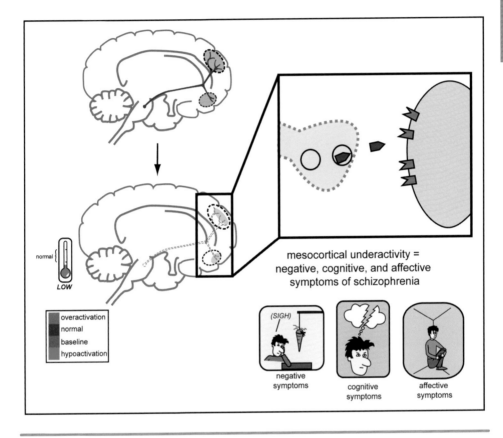

FIGURE 1.4. The mesocortical DA pathway is hypothetically also affected in schizophrenia. Here, DA cell bodies in the ventral tegmental area send projections to the DLPFC to regulate cognition and executive functions, and to the VMPFC to regulate emotions and affect. Hypoactivation of this pathway theoretically results in the negative, cognitive, and affective symptoms seen in schizophrenia. This hypothesis is sometimes called the "mesocortical DA hypothesis of negative, cognitive, and affective symptoms" of schizophrenia.

This DA deficit could result from ongoing degeneration due to glutamate excitotoxicity or from a neurodevelopmental impairment in the glutamatergic system.
Loss of motivation and interest, anhedonia, and lack of pleasure as observed in schizophrenia result not only from a malfunctioning mesocortical DA pathway but also from a deficient mesolimbic DA pathway.

Additional DA Pathways

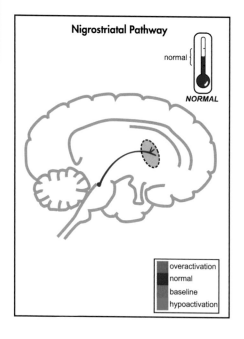

FIGURE 1.5. The nigrostriatal pathway sends DA projections from the substantia nigra to the striatum. This innervation of the basal ganglia regulates motor activity and is part of the extrapyramidal nervous system. A lack of DA here results in symptoms resembling Parkinson's disease, whereas an excess of DA will lead to hyperkinetic movement disorders such as dyskinesias.

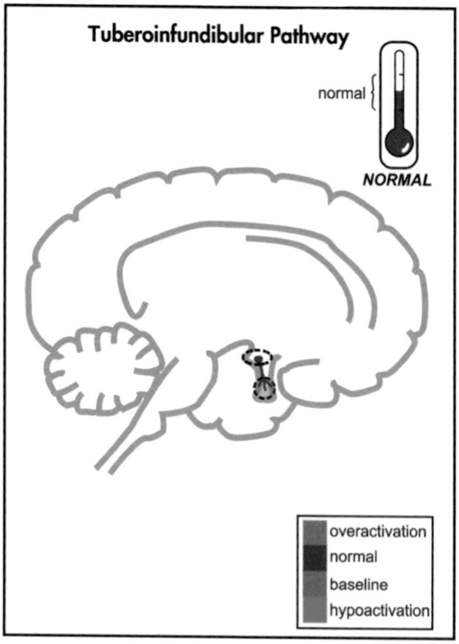

FIGURE 1.6. DA inhibits prolactin secretion via the tuberoinfundibular pathway as DA projections are sent from the hypothalamus to the anterior pituitary.

Although these two pathways are unaffected in schizophrenia, they do play an intricate part in the development of side effects, as they will not remain untouched by drugs interacting with DA neurons throughout the brain.

The Integrated DA Hypothesis of Schizophrenia

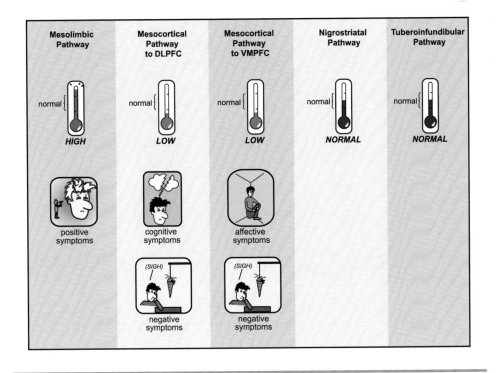

FIGURE 1.7. In schizophrenia, it appears that some DA pathways are overactive, others underactive, and others are functioning normally. Thus the DA system is neither "all too high," nor "all too low," but more precisely "out of tune," and DA needs to be increased in some areas, decreased in others, and left untouched in yet another set of circuits.

Various antipsychotic drugs acting at different receptor subtypes, especially blocking D2 receptors and serotonin 2A (5HT2A) receptors, might lead to that outcome.

Alternatively, regulating DA output by modulating transmitters such as glutamate may prove to be another way to "normalize" or "tune" DA circuits.

Key Glutamate Pathways

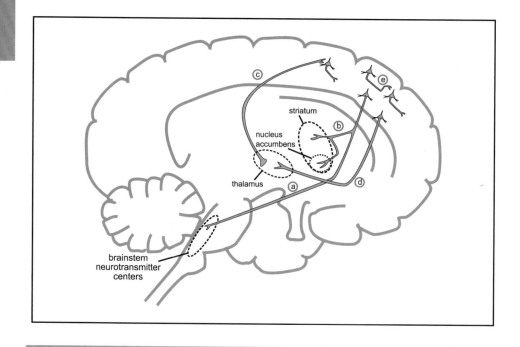

FIGURE 1.8. Similarly to DA, there are five glutamate pathways in the brain that are of particular relevance to schizophrenia.

(a) The <u>cortical brainstem glutamate projection</u> descends from layer 5 pyramidal neurons in the prefrontal cortex (PFC) to brainstem neurotransmitter centers, including the raphe (5HT), the locus coeruleus (norepinephrine), and the ventral tegmental area and substantia nigra (DA). This projection mainly regulates neurotransmitter release in the brainstem.

(b) The <u>cortico-striatal glutamate pathway</u> descends from the PFC to the striatum and the <u>cortico-accumbens glutamate pathway</u> sends projections to the nucleus accumbens. These pathways make up the "cortico-striatal" portion of cortico-striatal-thalamic loops.

(c) <u>Thalamo-cortical glutamate pathways</u> encompass pathways ascending from the thalamus and innervating pyramidal neurons in the cortex.

(d) <u>Cortico-thalamic glutamate pathways</u> descend from the PFC to the thalamus.

(e) The <u>cortico-cortical glutamatergic pathways</u> allow intracortical pyramidal neurons to communicate with each other.

NMDA Receptor Hypofunction Hypothesis of Schizophrenia

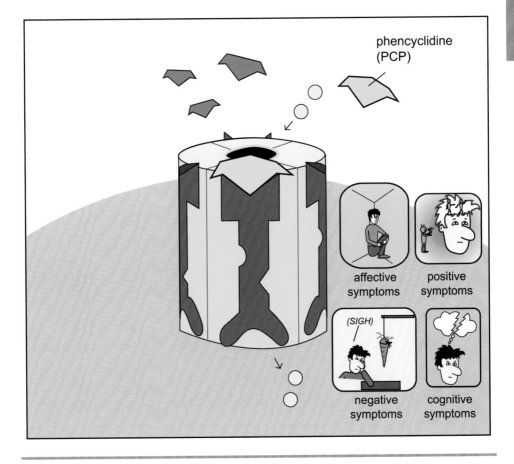

FIGURE 1.9. The NMDA (N-methyl-*d*-aspartate) receptor hypofunction hypothesis has been put forth in an attempt to explain mesolimbic DA hyperactivity. This hypothesis relies on the observation that when normal humans ingest phencyclidine (PCP), an NMDA receptor antagonist, they experience positive symptoms very similar to those observed in schizophrenia such as hallucinations and delusions.

Thus hypoactive glutamate NMDA receptors could theoretically explain the biological basis for the mesolimbic DA hyperactivity. PCP also induces affective symptoms such as blunted affect, negative symptoms such as social withdrawal, and cognitive symptoms such as executive dysfunction in normal humans. Hypofunctional NMDA receptors might therefore be involved in all symptoms of schizophrenia.

Role of Glutamate in the Mesolimbic System

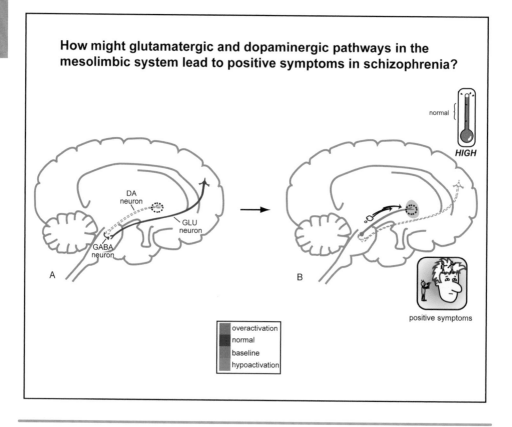

How might glutamatergic and dopaminergic pathways in the mesolimbic system lead to positive symptoms in schizophrenia?

FIGURE 1.10. Various theories have been put forth trying to explain the overactivity of the DA pathway in the mesolimbic system in schizophrenia. The descending cortico-brainstem glutamate pathway normally acts as a brake for the mesolimbic DA pathway, via gamma-aminobutyric acid (GABA) interneurons in the ventral tegmental area, leading to a tonic inhibition of the mesolimbic DA pathway (A). If glutamate projections become hypoactive, this tonic inhibition of the mesolimbic DA pathway will not occur, leading to hyperactivity in the mesolimbic DA pathway (B).

Role of Glutamate in the Mesocortical System

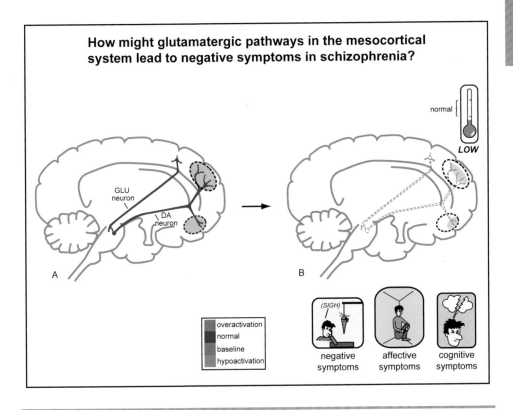

How might glutamatergic pathways in the mesocortical system lead to negative symptoms in schizophrenia?

FIGURE 1.11. Normally, the cortico-brainstem glutamate projections synapse directly onto DA neurons in the ventral tegmental area, where they tonically excite the mesocortical DA pathway and act as DA neuron accelerators (A).

Hypoactivity in glutamate projections, similarly to what is observed following PCP administration, can thus theoretically result in lost activation of the mesocortical DA neurons and might be the cause of the negative, cognitive, and affective symptoms seen in schizophrenia (B).

Key Serotonin Pathways

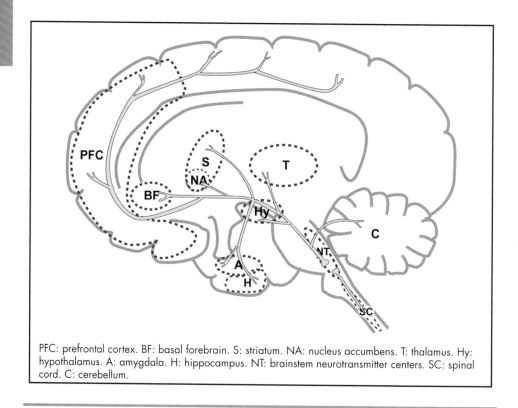

PFC: prefrontal cortex. BF: basal forebrain. S: striatum. NA: nucleus accumbens. T: thalamus. Hy: hypothalamus. A: amygdala. H: hippocampus. NT: brainstem neurotransmitter centers. SC: spinal cord. C: cerebellum.

FIGURE 1.12. In order to fully understand the properties of antipsychotics, it is imperative to examine the serotonin (5HT) pathways throughout the brain and how they modulate DA and glutamate circuits.

Ascending 5HT projections originate in the raphe nucleus in the brainstem and extend to many of the same regions as noradrenergic projections, with additional projections to the striatum and nucleus accumbens. These ascending projections may regulate mood, anxiety, sleep, and other functions. Descending 5HT projections extend down the brainstem and through the spinal cord and may regulate pain.

Opposing Actions of 5HT1A and 5HT2A Receptors on DA Release

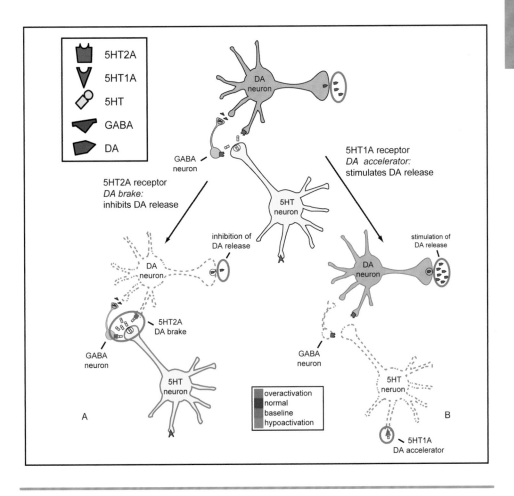

FIGURE 1.13. 5HT neurons can act on somatodendritic regions of DA neurons. Specifically, 5HT1A and 5HT2A receptors have opposite actions on DA release. Stimulation of 5HT1A receptors increases DA release, and thus 5HT1A receptors act as a DA accelerator. Stimulation of 5HT2A receptors inhibits DA release; thus 5HT2A receptors act as a DA brake. 5HT can regulate DA release directly or indirectly. (A) When 5HT binds to 5HT2A receptors on DA neurons or on GABA neurons, DA release is decreased directly or via inhibition through GABA release, respectively. (B) Upon binding to 5HT1A receptors, 5HT causes inhibition of its own release. A lack of 5HT results in disinhibition of DA release, and therefore increased DA output.

Somatodendritic Blockade of 5HT2A Receptors Leads to Increased DA Release

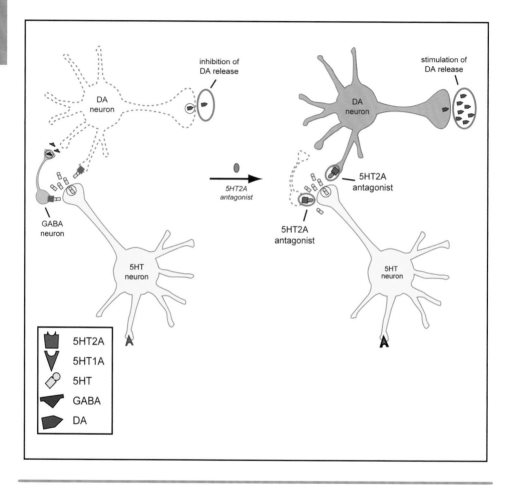

FIGURE 1.14. If stimulation of 5HT2A receptors leads to decreased DA release, then blocking 5HT2A receptors via antagonists should result in increased DA release.

Increasing DA release can therefore be obtained by either blocking 5HT2A receptors on postsynaptic DA neurons or by blocking 5HT2A receptors on GABA interneurons.

Regulation of DA Release by 5HT in the Nigrostriatal Pathway: Part 1

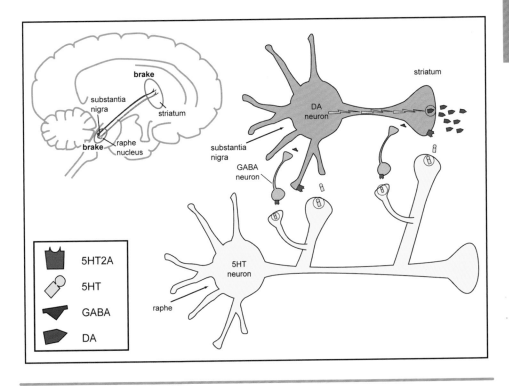

FIGURE 1.15. The 5HT-DA interaction at the level of the nigrostriatal pathway is important in mediating extrapyramidal side effects. Here 5HT can regulate DA release by acting on the somatodendritic regions of the DA neuron in the substantia nigra, or by acting on the axonal regions of the DA neuron in the striatum.

Part 1: In the absence of 5HT, DA is freely released in the striatum.

Regulation of DA Release by 5HT in the Nigrostriatal Pathway: Part 2

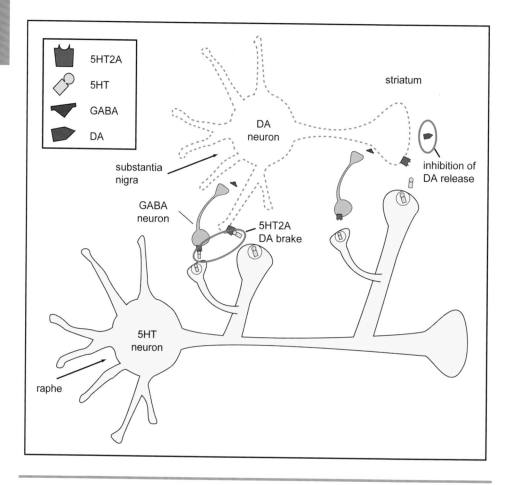

FIGURE 1.16. Part 2: When 5HT is released from raphe projections to the substantia nigra (red circle on the left), it will stimulate postsynaptic somatodendritic 5HT2A receptors on DA and GABA neurons.

This will lead to inhibition of axonal DA release (red circle on the right).

Regulation of DA Release by 5HT in the Nigrostriatal Pathway: Part 3

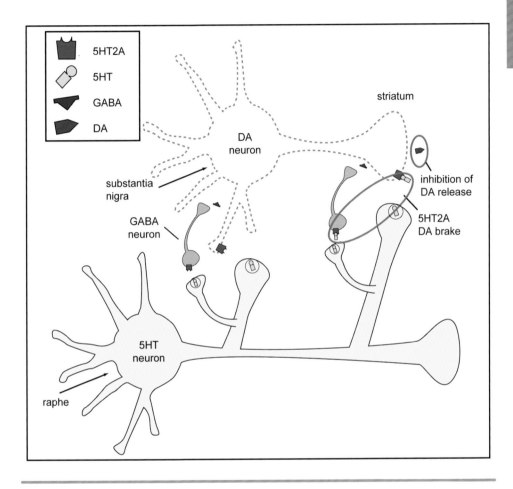

FIGURE 1.17. Part 3: When 5HT is released from a synaptic connection projecting from axoaxonal contacts or by volume neurotransmission between 5HT and DA axon terminals (red circle, bottom), it will stimulate postsynaptic 5HT2A receptors on DA and GABA neurons, leading to decreased axonal DA release (red circle, top).

What Happens at the Axon Terminal in the Striatum?

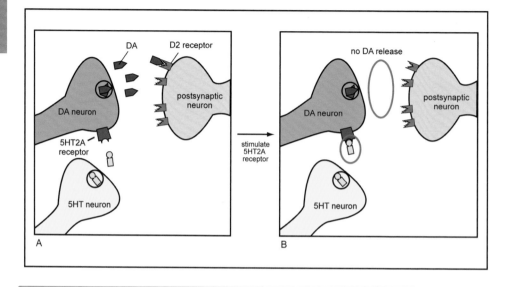

FIGURE 1.18. At the level of striatal axons, 5HT normally inhibits DA release. (A) In the absence of 5HT, however, DA is released without hindrance.

(B) In the presence of 5HT, 5HT2A receptors on DA terminals are stimulated, thus inhibiting DA release, thereby leading to a lack of synaptic DA.

5HT Also Modulates Cortical Glutamate Release

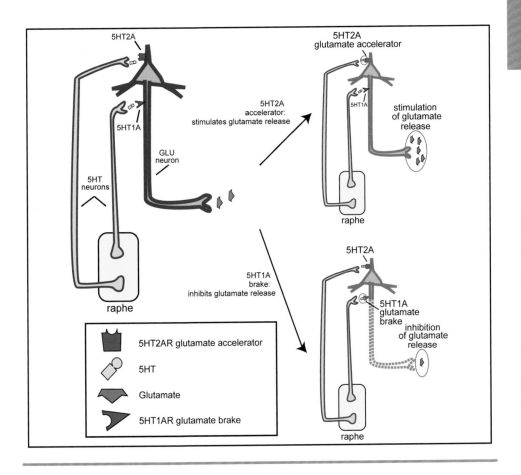

FIGURE 1.19. Stimulation of 5HT2A and 5HT1A receptors also leads to an opposing modulation of cortical glutamate release, but does so contrary to the actions of these same 5HT receptors upon DA release. Here, stimulation of 5HT2A receptors located on glutamate cell bodies induces an increase in glutamate release, acting as a glutamate accelerator. Stimulation of 5HT1A receptors located on glutamate axons inhibits glutamate release, acting as a glutamate brake.

As already mentioned, this is contrary to the regulation that 5HT has on DA release (see Figures 1.15–18), where stimulation of 5HT1A receptors leads to increased DA release (accelerator) and stimulation of 5HT2A receptors leads to inhibition of DA release (brake).

Strengthening the Signal-to-Noise Ratio in Schizophrenia

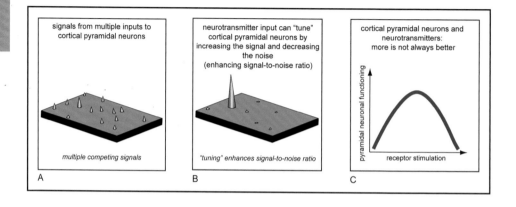

FIGURE 1.20. (A) Adequate information processing occurs when all neurotransmitters are working in tune. In schizophrenia, however, information processing in specific key brain areas is abnormal.

Prefrontal cortical activity in schizophrenia is not just "too high" or "too low," but it is most likely "out of tune" or "chaotic," with some areas hyperactive and others hypoactive.

(B) When prefrontal neurons are adequately tuned, the signal-to-noise ratio is sensitive enough to allow for proper filtering of "noise," resulting in the strengthening of one signal over another.

(C) As represented by the inverted U-shaped curve, moderation is preferable when it comes to receptor stimulation. Too much or too little stimulation is suboptimal. Thus in order to reach the optimal tuning of the signal-to-noise ratio it is important to determine where the system is on the curve, as it might need to be either increased or decreased.

— SECTION 1 —
Key Brain Regions and Their Hypothetical Functions: Relevance to Mood Disorders

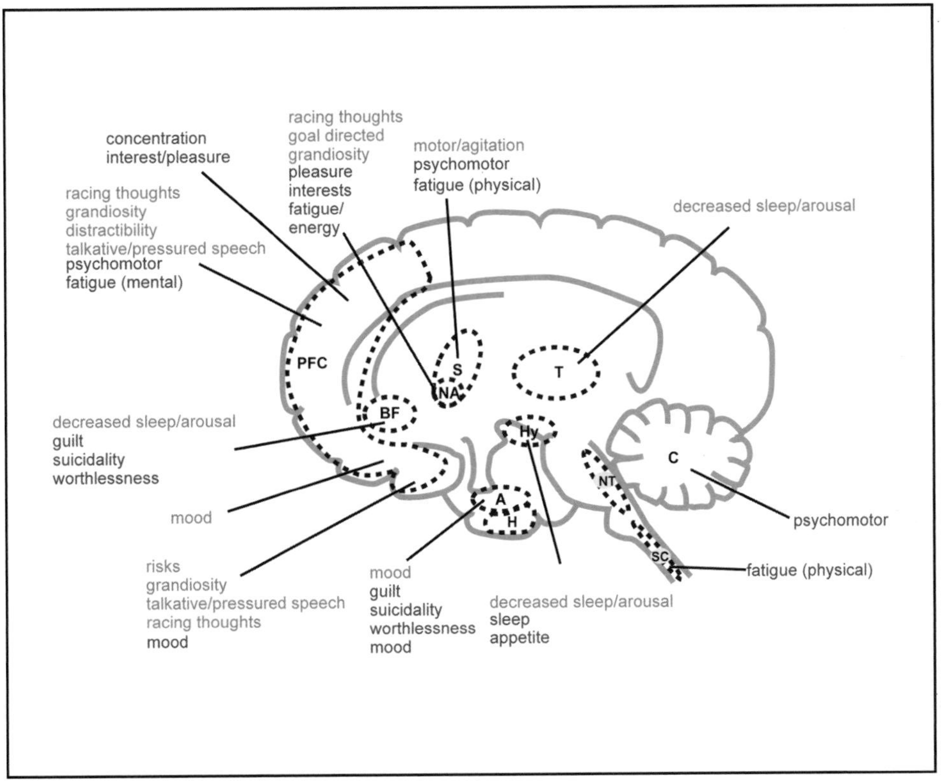

FIGURE 1.21. Similarly to what was seen for schizophrenia in Figure 1.1, various brain circuits are impaired in depression (blue text) and mania (red text). Hypo- or hyperactivity in these brain areas may hypothetically lead to aberrant neuronal activity and information processing, leading to the different presenting symptoms of depression.

Norepinephrine Pathways

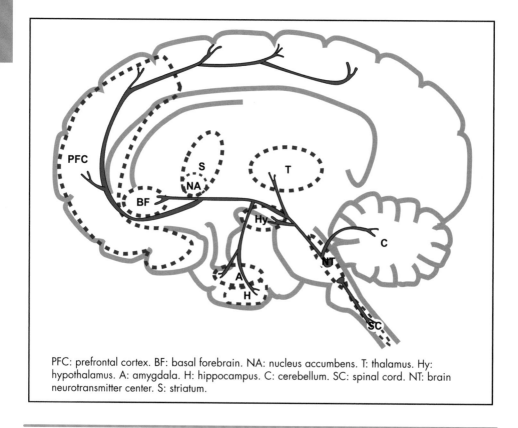

PFC: prefrontal cortex. BF: basal forebrain. NA: nucleus accumbens. T: thalamus. Hy: hypothalamus. A: amygdala. H: hippocampus. C: cerebellum. SC: spinal cord. NT: brain neurotransmitter center. S: striatum.

FIGURE 1.22. In section 1, the dopamine and serotonin pathways were introduced as the main regulators of schizophrenia. In addition to these two neurotransmitter pathways, norepinephrine also plays an integral part in mediating the symptoms of depression. Ascending projections originate from the locus coeruleus of brainstem to the cerebellum, thalamus, hypothalamus, basal forebrain, prefrontal cortex, amygdala, and hippocampus. Mood, arousal, and cognition are regulated and affected by norepinephrine. Descending projections from the spinal cord affect pain pathways.

Monoamine Hypothesis of Depression

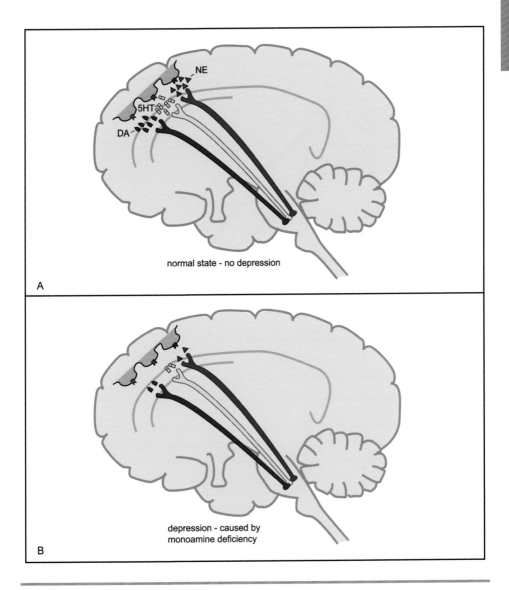

FIGURE 1.23. (A) Three monoamines are thought to be involved in the pathophysiology of depression and these include dopamine (DA), norepinephrine (NE), and serotonin (5HT). (B) The classical "monoamine hypothesis of depression" states that depression results from a deficiency in one or more of these three neurotransmitters.

Monoamine Receptor Hypothesis of Depression

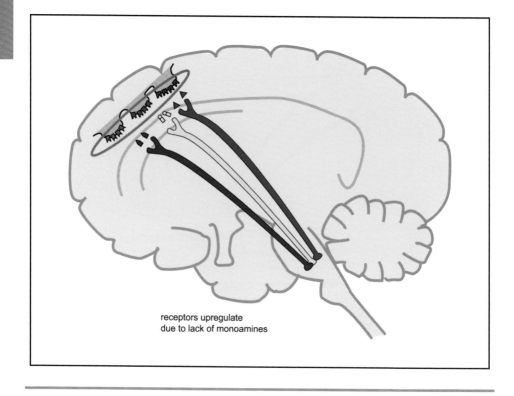

receptors upregulate
due to lack of monoamines

FIGURE 1.24. The monoamine receptor hypothesis builds on the classic monoamine hypothesis of depression by suggesting that decreased activity of monoamine neurotransmitters (dopamine, norepinephrine, and serotonin) causes upregulation of postsynaptic receptors (red circle) which may lead to depression. The monoamine receptor hypothesis suggests that if depression is caused by an upregulation of monoamine receptors, agents with antidepressant activity can act by ultimately downregulating monoamine receptors over time.

Time Course of Treatment in Depression

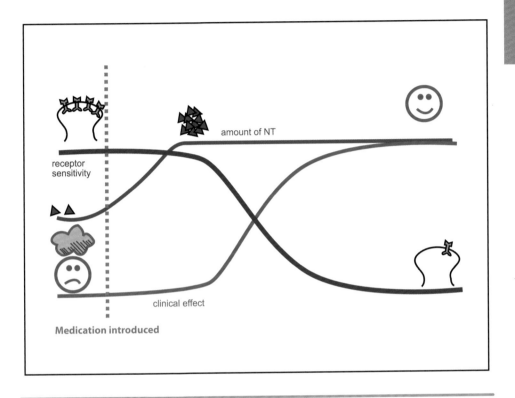

amount of NT

receptor
sensitivity

clinical effect

Medication introduced

FIGURE 1.25. Drugs with antidepressant activity have three time courses: one for clinical changes, a second one for neurotransmitter changes, and a third one for receptor sensitivity changes. While the neurotransmitter changes often occur rapidly after initial administration, clinical changes and receptor changes (i.e., down-regulation) take longer to occur. This observation has resulted in the hypothesis that neurotransmitter receptor sensitivity may mediate the clinical changes seen after medication administration, including the production of therapeutic antidepressant effects and the development of tolerance to side effects, all of which occur over a few weeks of time.

Norepinephrine Receptors

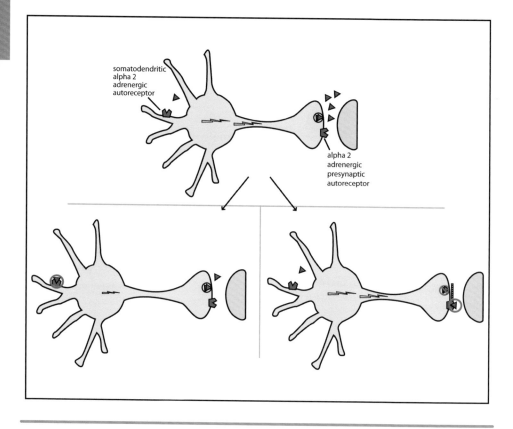

FIGURE 1.26. Presynaptic alpha 2 norepinephrine receptors (top neuron, receptors on the right) which are located on the axon terminals of norepinephrine neurons work as "gatekeepers" for their neurotransmitter. When norepinephrine builds up in the synapse and binds to alpha 2 receptors, the further release of norepinephrine is inhibited. These receptors aid in modulating the appropriate release of norepinephrine (bottom right figure, red circle). Presynaptic alpha 2 adrenergic receptors, which are located on the cell body and dendrites of a neuron, are termed somatodendritic autoreceptors (top neuron, receptors on the left). When norepinephrine binds to these somatodendritic autoreceptors (bottom left figure, red circle), this leads to a reduction in neuronal electrical activity leading to a shutdown of norepinephrine impulse flow and therefore a decrease in the amount of norepinephrine released at the synapse.

Serotonin Receptors

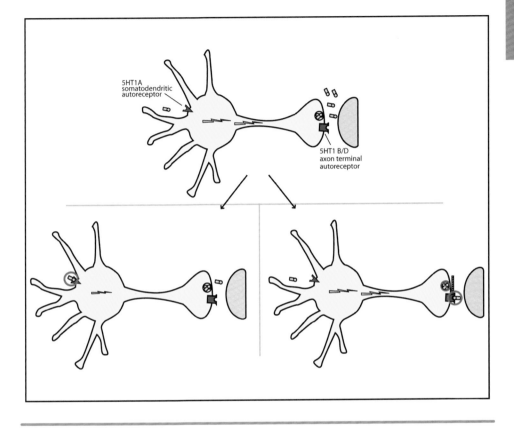

FIGURE 1.27. Similarly to presynaptic alpha 2 norepinephrine receptors, presynaptic 5HT1B/D receptors are located on the axon terminal of 5HT neurons (top neuron, receptors on the right) and act as "gatekeepers" for their neurotransmitter. When serotonin builds up in the synapse and binds to 5HT1B/D receptors, the further release of serotonin is inhibited. These receptors aid in modulating the appropriate release of serotonin (bottom right figure, red circle). Presynaptic 5HT1A somatodendritic autoreceptors (top neuron, receptors on the left), which are located on the cell body and dendrites of the serotonin neuron, work similarly to somatodendritic alpha 2 adrenergic receptors. When serotonin binds to these somatodendritic receptors (bottom left figure, red circle), this leads to a reduction in neuronal electrical activity leading to a shutdown of serotonin impulse flow and therefore a decrease in the amount of serotonin released at the synapse.

Dopamine Receptors

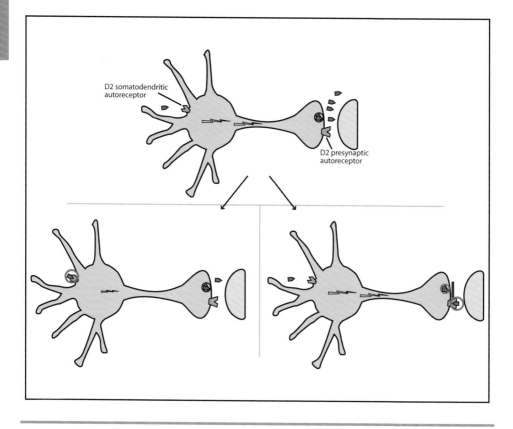

FIGURE 1.28. Similarly to presynaptic alpha 2 norepinephrine and 5HT1B/D receptors, presynaptic dopamine D2 receptors that are located on the axon terminal of dopamine neuron (top neuron, receptors on the right) work as "gatekeepers" for their neurotransmitter. When dopamine builds up in the synapse and binds to these D2 receptors, the further release of dopamine is inhibited. Thus these receptors aid in modulating the appropriate release of DA (bottom right figure, red circle). Presynaptic D2 somatodendritic autoreceptors, which are located on the cell body and dendrites of a dopamine neuron (top neuron, receptors on the left), work similarly to somatodendritic alpha 2 and 5HT1A receptors. When dopamine binds to these somatodendritic autoreceptors (bottom left figure, red circle), this leads to a reduction in neuronal electrical activity leading to a shutdown of dopamine impulse flow and therefore a decrease in the amount of dopamine released at the synapse.

Monoamine Interactions

A. Norepinephrine -- Serotonin

B. Serotonin -- Dopamine

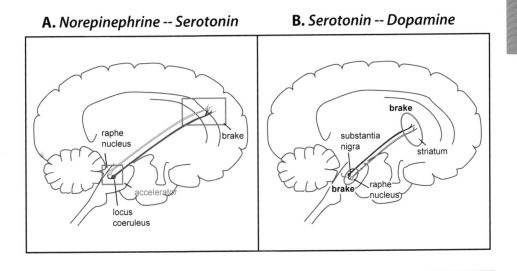

FIGURE 1.29. (A) Norepinephrine (NE) can boost serotonin (5HT) release via an excitatory input from the locus coeruleus projecting to the raphe and acting at alpha 1 receptors on serotonergic cell bodies and dendrites in the raphe (5HT accelerator; red box, bottom left). NE can also reduce 5HT release via an inhibitory input from NE nerve terminals acting at 5HT nerve terminals on alpha 2 receptors on 5HT axon terminals (5HT brake; red box, top right).

(B) In the nigrostriatal dopamine (DA) pathway, the release of 5HT acts as a brake on DA release. 5HT leads to inhibition of DA release, both at the level of DA cell bodies in the substantia nigra (red circle, bottom left) and at the level of axon terminals in the striatum (red circle, top right).

Appropriate Interplay Between Three Monoamines in Mood Disorders

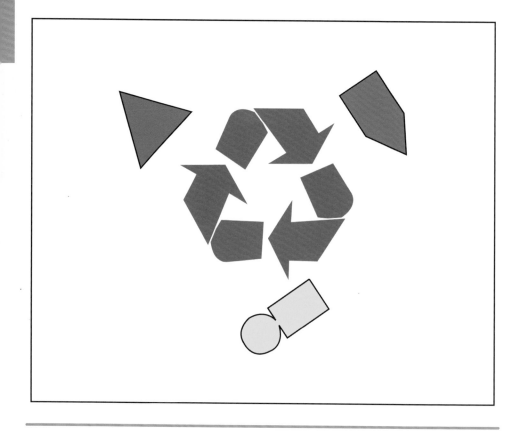

FIGURE 1.30. Adequate interplay of the three main monoamines is necessary for proper regulation of neurotransmitter release. The absence of neurotransmitters within the synaptic cleft is as detrimental as an overabundance of neurotransmitters, and thus a fine tuning needs to be reached to treat mood disorders.

Multifunctionality of Antipsychotics

The serendipitous discovery in the 1950s that the antihistamine chlorpromazine can relieve symptoms of psychosis led to the discovery of conventional antipsychotics. Their ability to block D2 receptors was recognized by the 1970s. Since then, much research has been done to improve antipsychotic medications. This chapter explores the different classes of antipsychotics, explains their mechanisms of action, and describes how they affect the brain circuitry in schizophrenia and in mood disorders.

Antipsychotics Overview

Class	Name
Conventional APs	Chlorpromazine, cyamemazine, fluphenthixol, fluphenazine, haloperidol, loxapine, mesoridazine, molindone, perphenazine, pimozide, pipothiazine, sulpiride, thioridazine, thiothixene, trifluoperazine, zuclopenthixol
SDAs	Clozapine, risperidone, paliperidone, olanzapine, quetiapine, ziprasidone, perospirone, zotepine, sertindole, low-dose loxapine?, low-dose cyamemazine?, iloperidone, asenapine
SDAs in development	SM13493/lurasidone, blonanserin, Y931, NRA0562, nemonapride
DPAs	Aripiprazole, low-dose sulpiride?, amisulpride?
DPAs in development	Bifeprunox, sarizotan, cariprazine (RGH188), 3PPP, SLV313, SLV314, ACR16, PNU 9639/OSU 6162, CI1007, ACP-104, SSR-181507
SPAs	SPA + SDA: ziprasidone, quetiapine, clozapine SDA + DPA + SPA: aripiprazole DPA + SPA: bifeprunox

AP: antipsychotic; SDA: serotonin 2A dopamine 2 antagonist; DPA: dopamine 2 partial agonist; SPA: serotonin 1A partial agonist

TABLE 2.1. Since the discovery of chlorpromazine in the 1950s, the development of new antipsychotics has been based mainly on their ability to block dopamine 2 receptors.

Additional properties have been integrated into the newer medications to improve therapeutic efficacy and prevent/reduce drug-related side effects. This table provides an overview of the different types of antipsychotics used to date.

– SECTION 1 –
Conventional D2 Antagonists

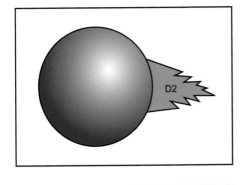

FIGURE 2.1. Conventional antipsychotics treat the symptoms of schizophrenia by blocking D2 receptors. Excessive blockade of D2 receptors, or blockade of DA receptors in hypoactive areas can lead to many side effects, including "neurolepsis," an extreme form of slowness or absence of motor movement, as well as the worsening of negative, cognitive, and affective symptoms.

Conventional Antipsychotics	
Generic Name	**Trade Name**
Chlorpromazine	Thorazine
Cyamemazine	Terican
Fluphenthixol	Depixol
Fluphenazine	Prolixin
Haloperidol	Haldol
Loxapine	Loxitane
Mesoridazine	Serentil
Molindone	Moban
Perphenazine	Trilafon
Pimozide	Orap
Pipothiazine	Piportil
Sulpiride	Dolmatil
Thioridazine	Mellaril
Thiothixene	Navane
Trifluoperazine	Stelazine
Zuclopenthixol	Clopixol

TABLE 2.2. Some of the conventional antipsychotics in use today.

D2 Antagonism in the Mesolimbic DA Pathway

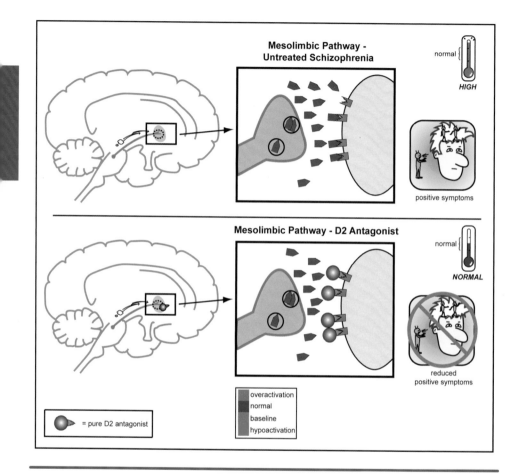

FIGURE 2.2. As excess DA release in the mesolimbic DA pathway leads to positive symptoms, it is necessary to reduce the actions of DA here in order to normalize the situation. Administration of a D2 blocker, such as any conventional antipsychotic, prevents DA from binding to the D2 receptor.

This D2 antagonism will lead to a reduction in both the hyperactivity of this pathway and the positive symptoms linked to it.

However, the mesolimbic DA pathway is not the only pathway affected by D2 antagonists.

D2 Antagonism in the Mesocortical DA Pathway

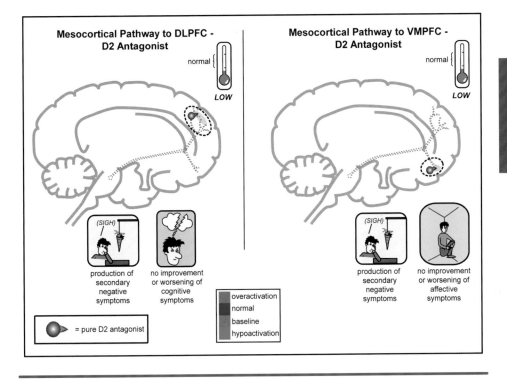

FIGURE 2.3. Administration of D2 blockers in the mesocortical pathway, however, is not wanted. Indeed, the hypoactivity of this pathway, which is related to cognitive symptoms (in the DLPFC), negative symptoms (in the DLPFC and VMPFC), and affective symptoms of schizophrenia (in the VMPFC) can actually be worsened by D2 blockade.

As the PFC does not have a high density of D2 receptors, the worsening of negative symptoms might also result from a deficient mesolimbic DA pathway.

In order to treat both positive and negative symptoms it is important to decrease DA activity in the mesolimbic pathway and increase DA tone in the mesocortical pathway. Dopamine function in schizophrenia is not simply "too high" or "too low;" it might be "out of tune." Thus today's psychopharmacologist needs to learn how to tune the system adequately.

D2 Antagonism in the Nigrostriatal DA Pathway

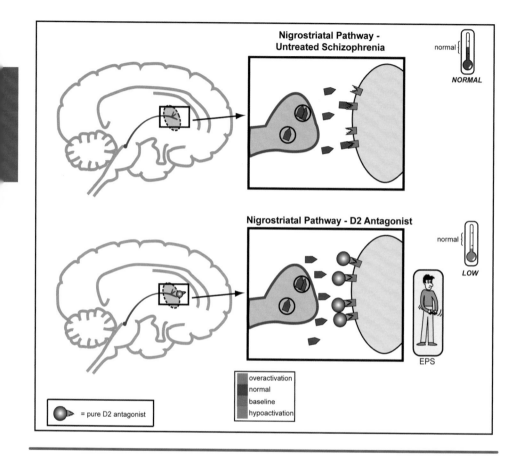

FIGURE 2.4. The nigrostriatal DA pathway, which is an integral part of the extrapyramidal nervous system, regulates motor control. This pathway appears to be relatively spared in schizophrenia; it does, however, induce the motor side effects seen after administration of conventional antipsychotics.

A lack of DA in this pathway results in movement disorders such as rigidity, akinesia, bradykinesia, and tremor, all hallmarks of Parkinson's disease.

A surplus of DA in this pathway, on the other hand, results in hyperkinetic movement disorders such as chorea and dyskinesia. Blockade of D2 receptors, such as with a conventional antipsychotic, prevents DA from binding there and can lead to motor side effects that are often collectively termed extrapyramidal side effects (EPS).

Consequences of
Chronic Receptor Blockade

Downregulation

Upregulation

FIGURE 2.5. The rate of synthesis of a receptor is controlled by intracellular enzymes relaying chemical instructions to the cell's DNA. When a protein kinase phosphorylates the transcription factor that tells the cell to slow down the synthesis of the neurotransmitter's receptor, it is called receptor downregulation. This slowing is exemplified by the red tortoise.

FIGURE 2.6. On the other hand, phosphorylation of a different transcription factor tells the cell to speed up synthesis of the neurotransmitter's receptor. This upregulation, which results in more receptors being expressed on the cell's surface and at a faster pace, is exemplified by the green hare.

Side Effects Due to Chronic D2 Blockade

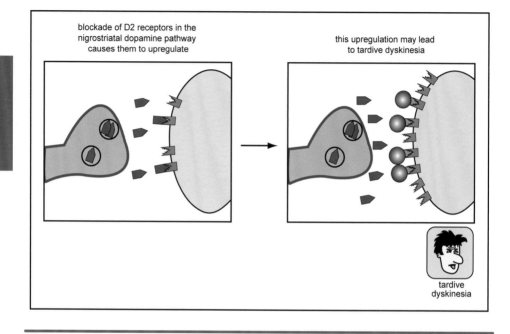

blockade of D2 receptors in the nigrostriatal dopamine pathway causes them to upregulate

this upregulation may lead to tardive dyskinesia

tardive dyskinesia

FIGURE 2.7. Long-term blockade of D2 receptors in the nigrostriatal DA pathway can lead to tardive dyskinesia, a hyperkinetic movement disorder characterized by facial and tongue movements (e.g., tongue protrusions, facial grimaces, chewing) as well as quick, jerky limb movements. Chronic administration of conventional antipsychotics can lead to D2 receptor supersensitivity, or upregulation, where an increase in receptor number attempts to overcome the drug-induced receptor blockade.

Every year, 5% of patients on conventional antipsychotics will develop tardive dyskinesia (25% of patients will be affected by 5 years), and for a disorder that starts in the early 20s, these odds are not acceptable.

Removing the conventional antipsychotic in time can prevent the occurrence of tardive dyskinesia, as this will allow the D2 receptors to lose their sensitivity and downregulate. However, if this is not done in time, irreversible molecular changes take place leading to tardive dyskinesia. Patients developing EPS early in their treatment appear more susceptible to tardive dyskinesia, and need to be monitored closely.

D2 Antagonism in the Tuberoinfundibular DA Pathway

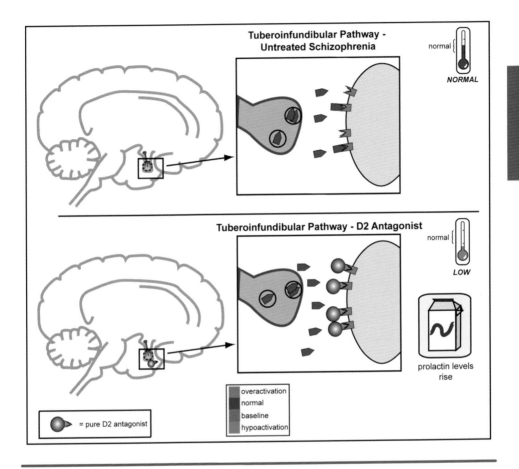

FIGURE 2.8. The tuberoinfundibular DA pathway projects from the hypothalamus to the pituitary gland, and tonically inhibits prolactin release. However, in the post-partum state, decreasing DA activity results in rising prolactin levels facilitating milk production during breast feeding.

Theoretically, the tuberoinfundibular DA pathway is "normal" in untreated schizo-phrenia. However, conventional antipsychotics reduce activity in this pathway, allow-ing prolactin levels to rise. Hyperprolactinemia ensues and is associated with side effects such as galactorrhea (breast secretions) and amenorrhea (irregular menstrual periods), as well as faster demineralization of bones in postmenopausal women. El-evated prolactin levels can also induce sexual dysfunction and weight gain.

Effects of D2 Antagonism on DA Circuitry: Part 1

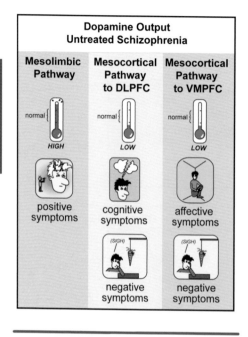

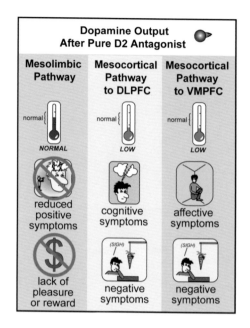

FIGURE 2.9. In untreated schizophrenia, DA output is high in the mesolimbic pathway, leading to positive symptoms, and low in the mesocortical pathways, leading to negative symptoms (projections to both DLPFC and VMPFC), cognitive symptoms (specifically the projections to the DLPFC), and affective symptoms (especially the projections to the VMPFC).

FIGURE 2.10. A D2 antagonist reduces DA output indiscriminately throughout the brain. While positive symptoms of psychosis will be successfully reduced, the experience of pleasure also mediated by the mesolimbic DA pathway will be impaired. The near shut-down of the mesolimbic DA pathway necessary to improve positive symptoms can lead to anhedonia and apathy. Decreasing DA output in the hypoactive mesocortical pathways will further reduce this pathway's activity and can actually worsen cognitive, negative, or affective symptoms.

Effects of D2 Antagonism on DA Circuitry: Part 2

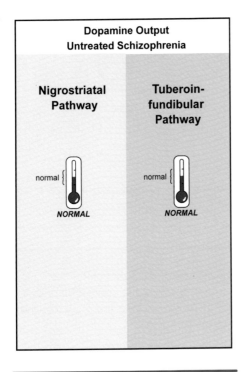

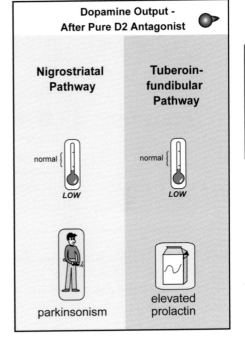

FIGURE 2.11. Unlike what is hypothesized for the mesolimbic and mesocortical pathways, DA output is theoretically normal in the nigrostriatal and tuberoinfundibular pathways. Thus, it would make sense that one would not want to alter the normal activity in these pathways when treating schizophrenia.

FIGURE 2.12. By reducing DA output in the nigrostriatal pathway, D2 antagonists can lead to EPS and tardive dyskinesia. Chronic DA blockade of the tuberoinfundibular pathway will result in hyperprolactinemia and its accompanying complications.

Tight and Long-Lasting Binding of Conventional Antipsychotics

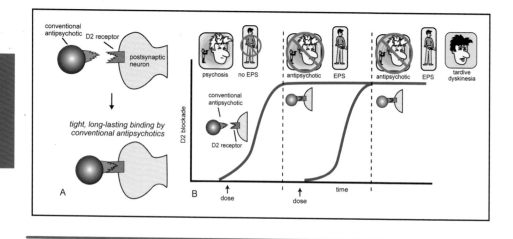

FIGURE 2.13. (A) When conventional antipsychotics bind to D2 receptors, this binding is tight and long-lasting. The teeth on the binding site of the conventional antipsychotic bind tightly to the grooves of the D2 receptor, locking the drug into the receptor binding site and blocking it in a long-lasting manner.

(B) In the absence of D2 receptor blockade, a patient with schizophrenia exhibits positive symptoms of psychosis such as delusions and hallucinations, but does not have EPS. In the presence of a conventional antipsychotic, D2 receptor blockade is very tight, leading to both antipsychotic action and EPS. Following addition of a second dose of a conventional antipsychotic, the D2 receptor blockade remains in place. Thus antipsychotic actions that result from conventional antipsychotics are continuously associated with EPS and can eventually lead to tardive dyskinesia.

Additional Side Effects of Conventional Antipsychotics

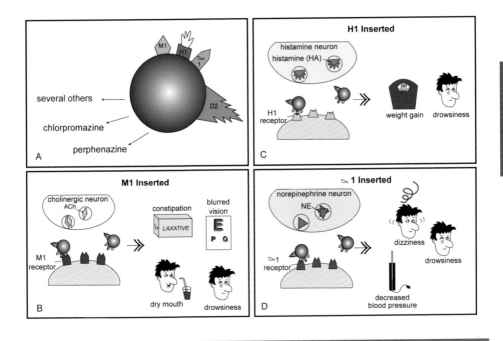

FIGURE 2.14. (A) Besides blockade at D2 receptors, conventional antipsychotics have additional pharmacologic properties: blockade of M1 muscarinic cholinergic receptors, blockade of H1 histamine receptors, and blockade of alpha1 adrenergic receptors. These induce side effects common to all drugs with this receptor profile.

(B) The M1 muscarinic anticholinergic portion of the drug can lead to constipation, blurred vision, dry mouth, and drowsiness when binding to acetylcholine receptors.

(C) The H1 histamine portion of the drug can lead to drowsiness and weight gain.

(D) The alpha1 adrenergic portion of the drug can lead to dizziness, decreased blood pressure, and drowsiness.

The Conventional Antipsychotic Haloperidol

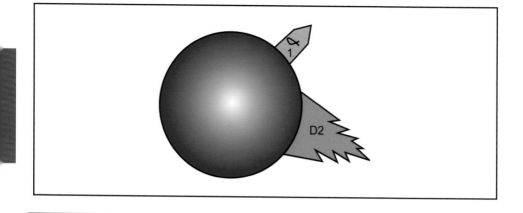

FIGURE 2.15. Haloperidol, one of the most commonly used conventional antipsychotics, has relatively weak cholinergic and histaminergic binding activity but exhibits substantial inhibition at alpha1 adrenergic receptors.

Although they are very efficacious at reducing positive symptoms, conventional antipsychotics are plagued with side effects and thus their use has decreased over time. The propensity of conventional antipsychotics to induce EPS is one of the main reasons that most psychopharmacologists stay away from these medications. However, even within this class of drugs there are differences. Varying degrees of blockade at the muscarinic cholinergic receptors, for example, will lead to different amounts of EPS, such that weak anticholinergic activity induces more EPS and strong anticholinergic activity leads to less severe EPS.

Cholinergic Side Effects of Antipsychotics: Part 1

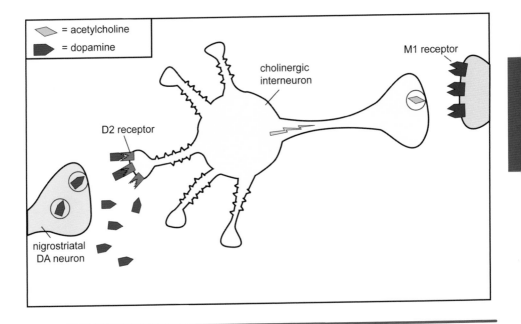

FIGURE 2.16. DA and acetylcholine have a reciprocal relationship in the nigrostriatal DA pathway.

Normally, when DA is released onto cholinergic dendrites it stimulates D2 receptors, and acetylcholine release is suppressed.

Cholinergic Side Effects of Antipsychotics: Part 2

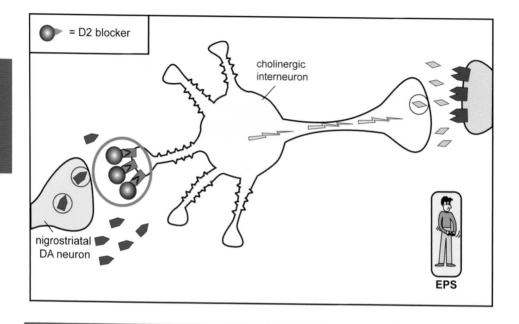

FIGURE 2.17. Blockade of D2 receptors by conventional antipsychotics removes the inhibitory action of DA on the cholinergic neurons (red circle on the left) and leads to increased acetylcholine release (pink acetylcholine on the right).

The resulting increased stimulation of postsynaptic cholinergic receptors is correlated with the induction of EPS.

Cholinergic Side Effects of Antipsychotics: Part 3

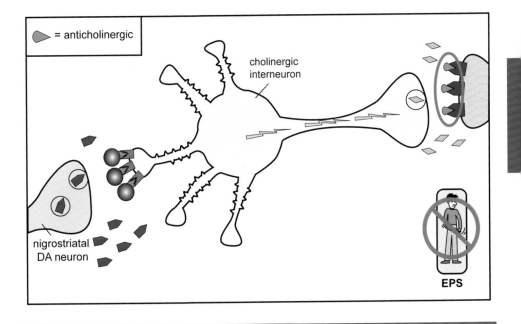

FIGURE 2.18. Thus it appears that EPS can be induced in a system where DA is low and acetylcholine is high. Blocking the overactive acetylcholine release with an M1 receptor antagonist for example (anticholinergic, circle on the right) will compensate for the increased acetylcholine release induced by D2 receptor blockade. This will thus decrease or prevent the occurrence of EPS.

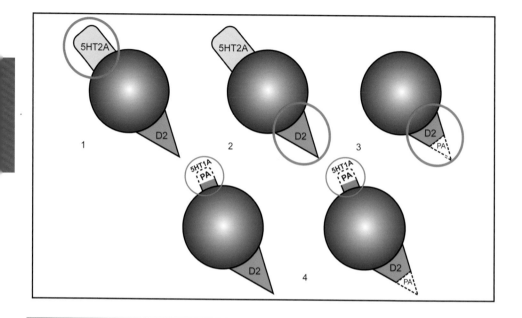

FIGURE 2.19. Atypical antipsychotics represent the second generation of antipsychotics. They are distinguished from conventional antipsychotics by their clinical properties (low EPS and good efficacy for negative symptoms), as well as by four pharmacological characteristics:

(1) Atypical antipsychotics couple their D2 antagonism with 5HT2A antagonism.

(2) The dissociation rate at the D2 receptor sets apart the "atypicality" of an antipsychotic. Tight and long-lasting binding is characteristic of conventional antipsychotics, whereas rapid dissociation is a feature of atypical antipsychotics.

(3) Atypical antipsychotics can also be D2 partial agonists (DPAs). These agents bind in a manner that is neither too antagonizing nor too stimulating, allowing for just the "right" amount of neurotransmission at D2 receptors.

(4) Full or partial agonism at the 5HT1A receptor can also be a characteristic of some atypical antipsychotics. Stimulation at the 5HT1A receptor can increase DA release, thus improving affective, cognitive, and negative symptoms while reducing the risk of EPS and prolactin elevation. Serotonin1A agonism can also decrease glutamate release, which may indirectly reduce the positive symptoms of psychosis.

Rapid Dissociation Theory of Atypical Antipsychotic Action

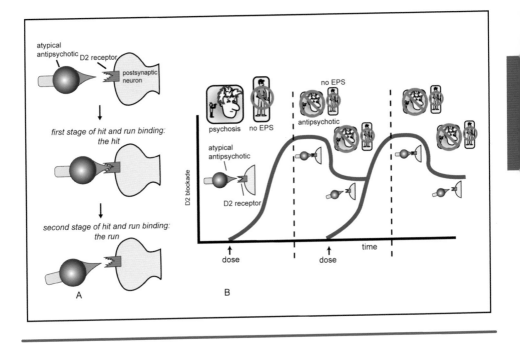

FIGURE 2.20. (A) Unlike conventional antipsychotics, atypical antipsychotics do not have teeth on their binding site, and thus they cannot be locked into position upon binding to D2 receptors. Atypical antipsychotics interact loosely with D2 receptors, exemplified by their smooth binding site. This results in a rapid dissociation from the binding site, also referred to as the "hit and run" receptor binding property. Thus during the "hit," the atypical antipsychotic does not get locked into the receptor binding site and is able to "run" and slip away easily.

(B) An untreated patient with schizophrenia exhibits positive symptoms but no EPS. Upon administration of an atypical antipsychotic, the D2 receptors get blocked for only a short period of time, in contrast to the long-lasting blockade from conventional antipsychotics. Only short blockade of D2 receptors is theoretically required for antipsychotic action, whereas persistent blockade of D2 receptors is required for EPS to occur. Atypical antipsychotics are beneficial in treating the positive symptoms of schizophrenia while preventing EPS, as dose after dose, they bind just long enough to D2 receptors to induce antipsychotic effects, but they "run away" before eliciting EPS.

Effects of Rapid D2 Dissociation on DA Circuitry: Part 1

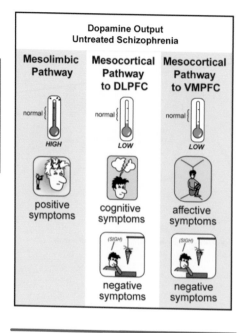

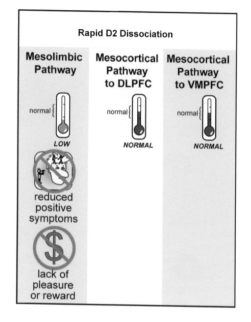

FIGURE 2.21. In untreated schizophrenia, DA output is high in the mesolimbic pathway, leading to positive symptoms, and low in the mesocortical pathways, leading to negative symptoms (projections to both DLPFC and VMPFC), cognitive symptoms (specifically the projections to the DLPFC), and affective symptoms (especially the projections to the VMPFC).

FIGURE 2.22. Administration of an agent that rapidly dissociates from D2 receptors leads to a reduced DA output in the mesolimbic DA pathway, thus decreasing positive symptoms. Unfortunately, decreasing DA output in this pathway can also lower the experiences of pleasure and reward. Loose binding of atypical antipsychotics in the mesocortical DA pathway could potentially reset this pathway. Theoretically, persistent blockade of D2 receptors is needed in this pathway to worsen affective, cognitive, or negative symptoms. Thus rapid blockade of and dissociation from D2 receptors in the mesocortical pathway may not lead to these side effects.

Effects of Rapid D2 Dissociation on DA Circuitry: Part 2

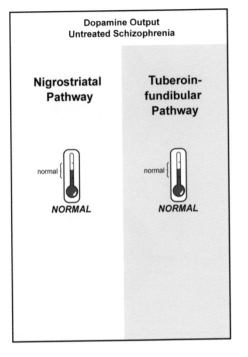

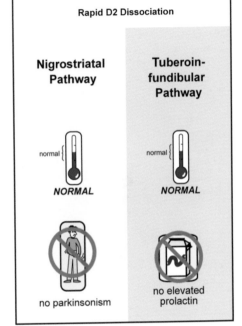

FIGURE 2.23. Unlike what is hypothesized for the mesolimbic and mesocortical pathways, DA output is theoretically normal in the nigrostriatal and tuberoinfundibular pathways. Thus it would make sense that one would not want to alter the normal activity in these pathways when treating schizophrenia.

FIGURE 2.24. In the nigrostriatal and tuberoinfundibular DA pathways, administration of agents that rapidly dissociate from D2 receptors may exhibit reduced risk for EPS and may not lead to elevated prolactin levels.

Pharmacological Profile of Atypical Antipsychotics

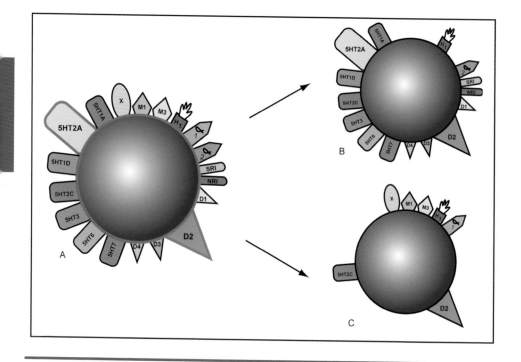

FIGURE 2.25. One characteristic of atypical antipsychotics is their vast pharmacological profile. (A) Besides being D2 and 5HT2A blockers, they interact with more receptors of the DA and 5HT family, such as 5HT1A, 5HT1D, 5HT2C, 5HT3, 5HT6, and 5HT7 receptors; the 5HT transporter; and D1, D3, and D4 receptors. They also interact with receptors of other neurotransmitters, such as the norepinephrine transporter and the muscarinic 1 and 3, histamine 1, and alpha 1 and 2 adrenergic receptors. Receptor "X" represents the unclear actions that some atypical antipsychotics have on the insulin system, where they change cellular insulin resistance and increase fasting plasma triglyceride levels.

While some of the different pharmacological properties of atypical antipsychotics contribute to their therapeutic effects (B), others can actually elicit side effects (C).

No two atypical antipsychotics have identical binding properties, which probably helps to explain how they all have somewhat distinctive clinical properties.

Atypical 5HT2A/D2 Antipsychotics:
Overview

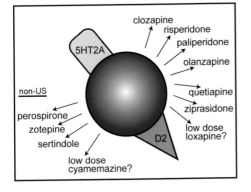

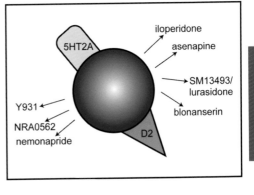

FIGURE 2.26. Presented in this figure are the atypical antipsychotics that are 5HT2A/D2 antagonists, including clozapine, risperidone, paliperidone, olanzapine, quetiapine, and ziprasidone in the United States, as well as perospirone, zotepine, and sertindole in other countries. Loxapine and cyamemazine may also be considered 5HT2A/D2 antagonists when given at low doses.

FIGURE 2.27. New 5HT2A/D2 antagonists are currently in development; these include iloperidone, asenapine, SM13493/lurasidone, blonanserin, nemonapride, NRA0562, and Y931.

Combined 5HT2A/D2 Receptor Blockade Leads to Less EPS

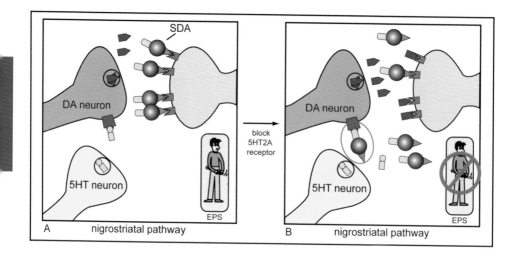

FIGURE 2.28. When postsynaptic D2 receptors are blocked by antagonists, especially long-term, this can result in the occurrence of EPS. This can also occur with 5HT2A/D2 antagonists if only the DA blocking property is active, as represented in (A).

When both D2 and 5HT2A receptors are blocked by SDAs, then the 5HT2A blockade actually opposes the actions of the D2 blockade. Blocking 5HT2A receptors leads to increased DA release, as 5HT normally inhibits DA release (B).

Increased levels of DA in the synapse will then compete with the SDAs for the D2 receptors on the postsynaptic neurons, thus preventing full inhibition. Reversal of D2 blockade therefore prevents the occurrence of EPS, similarly to what is seen in compounds with rapid D2 dissociation.

Effects of 5HT2A Blockade in the Mesocortical DA Pathway

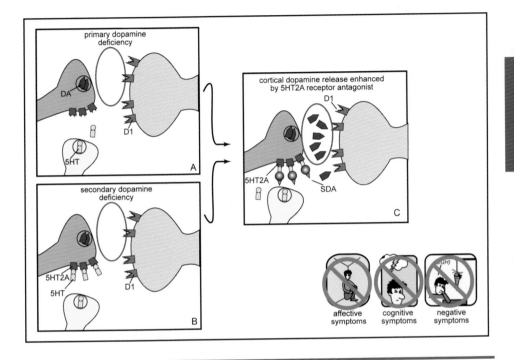

FIGURE 2.29. Affective, cognitive, and negative symptoms are thought to be the result of a lack of DA stimulation in the mesocortical pathway. DA deficiency could be primary (A) or secondary (B) due to excess release of 5HT (5HT inhibits DA release).

Blockade of 5HT2A receptors following administration of SDAs should actually lead to increased synaptic DA levels, which could compensate for the DA deficiency and relieve affective, cognitive, and negative symptoms (C).

Indirect Regulation of Mesolimbic DA Pathway by 5HT2A Blockade in the Cortex

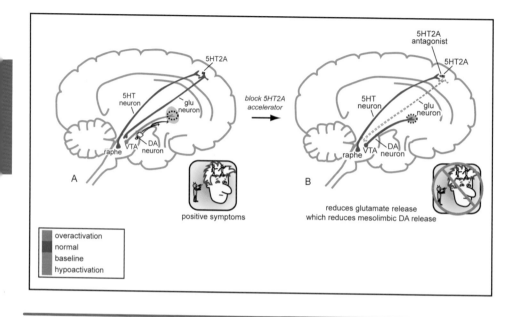

FIGURE 2.30. 5HT2A receptor stimulation can also indirectly regulate DA activity in the mesolimbic DA pathway. 5HT projections from the raphe synapse onto cortical glutamate projections that synapse onto DA projections in the VTA.

(A) Normally, released 5HT stimulates 5HT2A receptors on cortical glutamate projections. This leads to stimulation of these projections and thus excitation of DA neurons in the VTA, possibly resulting in the positive symptoms of schizophrenia.

(B) By blocking 5HT2A receptors in the cortex, glutamate release is reduced in the VTA and thus the excitation of DA neurons in the VTA is also decreased. Antagonizing 5HT2A receptors in the cortex can therefore possibly be used to block the positive symptoms of schizophrenia.

Prolactin Regulation by DA and 5HT

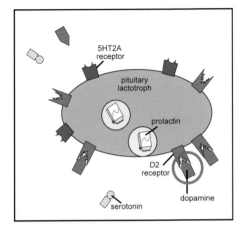 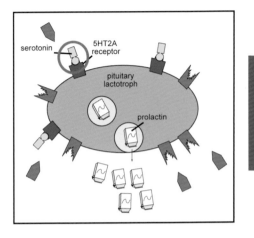

FIGURE 2.31. How do DA and 5HT normally regulate prolactin secretion in the tuberoinfundibular pathway? Under normal conditions, DA is inhibitory to prolactin release from pituitary lactotroph cells by binding to D2 receptors in the pituitary gland (red circle).

FIGURE 2.32. On the other hand, when 5HT binds to 5HT2A receptors on pituitary lactotroph cells, prolactin release is increased (red circle). Thus, 5HT and DA regulate prolactin release in an opposing manner.

Effects of Conventional vs. Atypical 5HT2A/D2 Antipsychotics on Prolactin Release

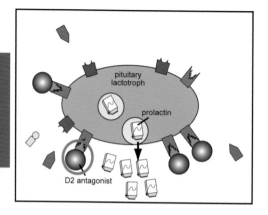

FIGURE 2.33. Due to their antagonism at D2 receptors, conventional antipsychotics block the inhibitory action that DA has on prolactin, and therefore lead to increased prolactin release.

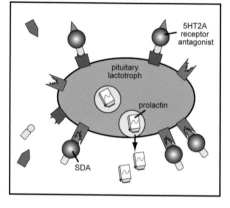

FIGURE 2.34. Atypical antipsychotics such as 5HT2A/D2 antagonists have no net effect on prolactin release and allow normal levels of prolactin to be secreted. Whereas blocking D2 receptors increases prolactin release, blocking 5HT2A receptors blocks the D2-induced release of prolactin. Thus antagonism at one receptor subtype cancels the action of blocking the other receptor, and no net change is observed in prolactin release.

Effects of 5HT2A/D2 Antagonism on DA Circuitry: Part 1

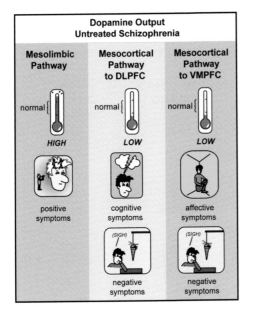

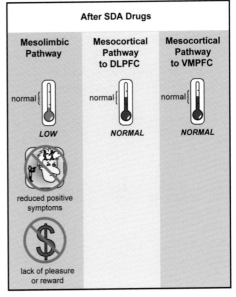

FIGURE 2.35. In untreated schizophrenia, DA output is high in the mesolimbic pathway, leading to positive symptoms, and low in the mesocortical pathways, leading to negative symptoms (projections to both DLPFC and VMPFC), cognitive symptoms (specifically the projections to the DLPFC), and affective symptoms (especially the projections to the VMPFC).

FIGURE 2.36. Administration of a 5HT2A/D2 antagonist decreases the DA output in the mesolimbic DA pathway, thereby reducing the positive symptoms of psychosis. Unfortunately this action may also reduce the experience of pleasure or reward, which is also mediated by that pathway. 5HT2A antagonism can offset a decrease in mesocortical DA resulting from D2 blockade and result in a net increase in DA output in that pathway, thereby treating the cognitive, affective, and negative symptoms of schizophrenia.

Effects of 5HT2A/D2 Antagonism on DA Circuitry: Part 2

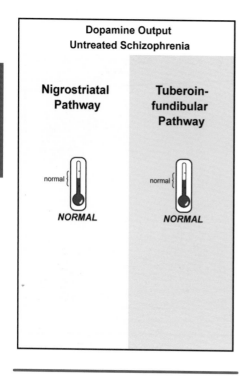

FIGURE 2.37. Unlike what is hypothesized for the mesolimbic and mesocortical pathways, DA output is theoretically normal in the nigrostriatal and tuberoinfundibular pathways. Thus it would make sense that one would not want to alter the normal activity in these pathways when treating schizophrenia.

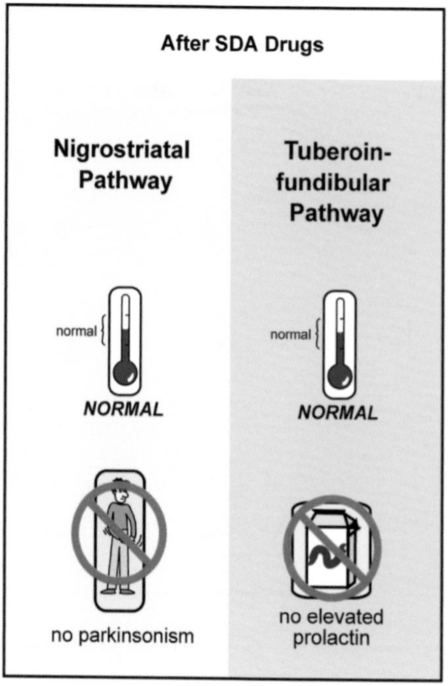

FIGURE 2.38. The net result of blocking 5HT2A and D2 receptors in the nigrostriatal and tuberoinfundibular pathways could be a normalization of the DA output, thus eliminating the risks of the development of EPS and preventing the increase in prolactin levels.

− SECTION 3 −
The Theory Behind Partial Agonists

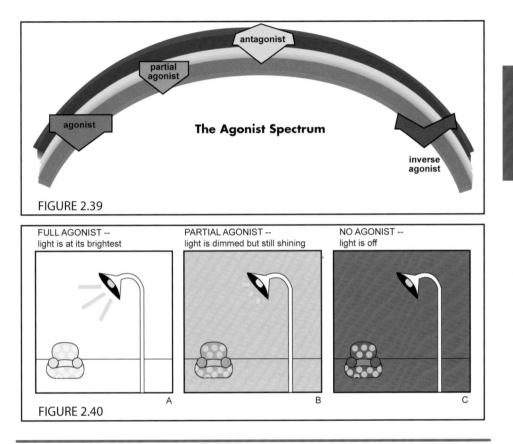

FIGURE 2.39

FIGURE 2.40

FIGURE 2.39. Naturally occurring neurotransmitters that stimulate receptors are agonists; thus drugs that stimulate receptors are also called agonists. Drugs that stimulate a receptor to a lesser degree are partial agonists or stabilizers. Antagonists are "silent" and do not have an action of their own; they only block the action of agonists. Inverse agonists can block the actions of the agonist, or they can reduce baseline activity in the absence of an agonist.

FIGURE 2.40. A light controlled by a rheostat is a good analogy for the concept of the agonist spectrum. The room is brightest when the light is fully on, as after a full agonist (A). A partial agonist will lead to a partially lit room, either by acting as a "net agonist" turning the lights partially on, or by acting as a "net antagonist" and dimming the light of an agonist (B). In the absence of an agonist or partial agonist, the room is dark, and the light is off (C).

The Agonist Spectrum of the Signal Transduction Pathway

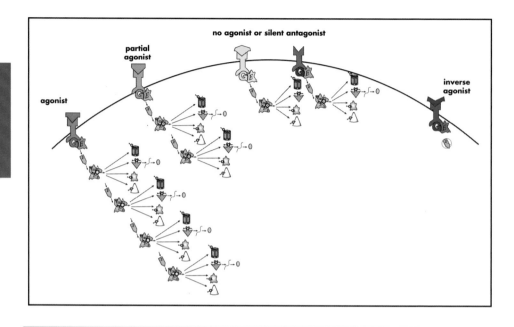

FIGURE 2.41. The concept of the agonist spectrum can also be adapted to the G protein-linked signal transduction system. Whereas a full agonist leads to maximal signal transduction, a partial agonist leads only to a level of signal transduction between the full agonist and no agonist. Antagonists have no effect on signal transduction by themselves, but reduce the level of signal transduction caused by an agonist.

Inverse agonists, on the other hand, can actually lead to lower levels of signal transduction than that which is normally produced in the absence of an agonist.

How Is the DA Spectrum Related to Receptor Output?

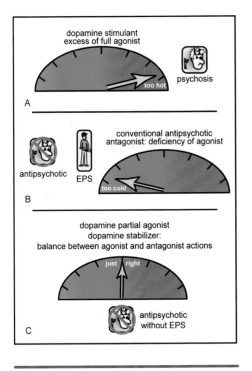

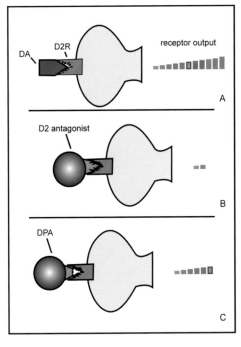

FIGURE 2.42. In order to understand the actions of DA and DA agents within an agonist spectrum, it may be helpful to look at them along a "hot-cold" spectrum. That is, DA acts as the ultimate agonist and is too "hot," resulting in psychosis (A). D2 blockers such as conventional antagonists are too "cold," and while they prevent psychotic episodes they also lead to EPS (B). Partial agonists are "lukewarm," leading to just the right stimulation of DA receptors, thus preventing psychotic episodes without inducing EPS (C).

FIGURE 2.43. DA is the ultimate full agonist, leading to full receptor output (A). At the other end of the spectrum, conventional antipsychotics (full antagonists) lead to only very little DA output (B). The atypical antipsychotics that have 5HT2A/D2 blocking activity lead to similarly little DA output. D2 partial agonists (DPAs), on the other hand, stimulate DA receptors only partially, leading to an intermediate or moderate DA output (C).

How Do Partial Agonists Lead to Second Messenger Activation?

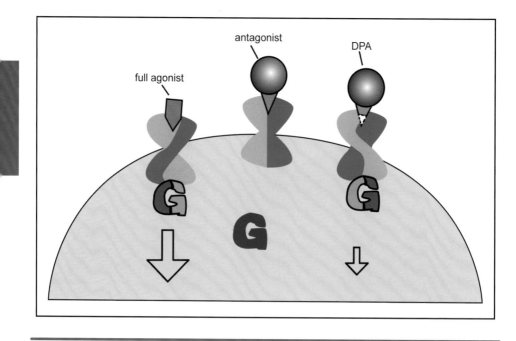

FIGURE 2.44. Similarly the actions of compounds along the agonist spectrum can be seen at the level of the second messenger system. A full agonist results in the full conformational change of the receptor, inducing maximal activation of the G protein-linked signal transduction cascade. An antagonist prevents binding of the G protein to the receptor, and thus prevents second messenger activation.

A DA partial agonist results in a conformational change of the receptor leading to partial second messenger activation. The second messenger activation by the partial agonist is only a fraction of the activation resulting from a full agonist.

Antipsychotics Along the Agonist Spectrum

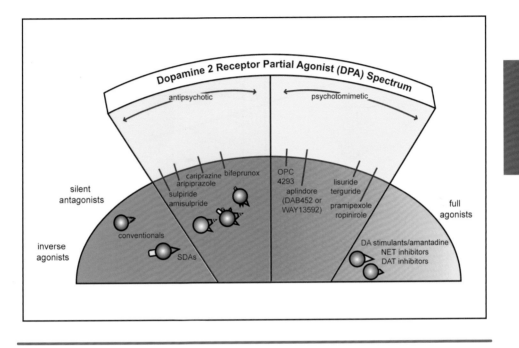

FIGURE 2.45. Atypical antipsychotics also fall within the agonist spectrum, ranging from inverse agonist to full agonist. Some atypical antipsychotics specifically fall within the partial agonist sector of this full agonist spectrum. Too much agonism resembles a psychotomimetic, which is unfavorable in the treatment of schizophrenia.

Partial agonists that lie closer to the antagonist side of the spectrum are favored, and some exhibit good antipsychotic efficacy, such as aripiprazole. Other agents, such as amisulpride and sulpiride, may exhibit partial agonist properties at low doses.

D2 Partial Agonists: Overview

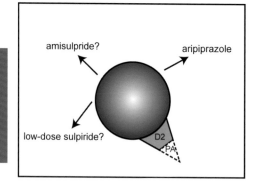

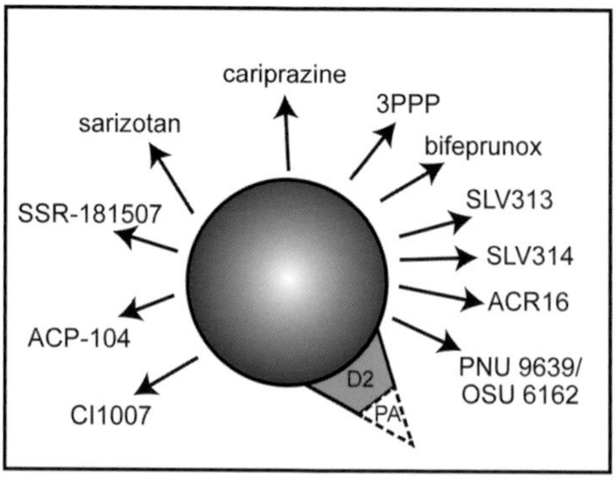

FIGURE 2.46. There is currently one well characterized DA partial agonist (DPA) on the market: aripiprazole. Although not well characterized, amisulpride and sulpiride may also act as partial agonists, especially at low doses.

FIGURE 2.47. DA partial agonists are potentially effective antipsychotics. Many are currently in development, including cariprazine, 3PPP, bifeprunox, SLV313, SLV314, ACR16, PNU 9639/OSU 6162, CI1007, ACP-104, SSR-181507, and sarizotan.

The Benefits of Partial DA Output

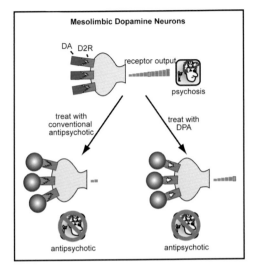

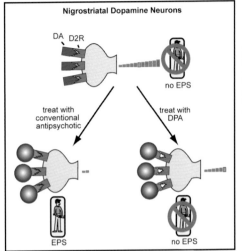

FIGURE 2.48. Excessive DA stimulation in the mesolimbic DA pathway theoretically results in psychosis. Similarly to conventional antipsychotics, DA partial agonists block D2 receptors in the mesolimbic DA pathway, thus preventing the excessive DA output from mesolimbic DA neurons that leads to psychosis. Even though DA partial agonists do not reduce DA output as strongly as conventional antipsychotics, their action is sufficient to attain similar antipsychotic efficacy.

FIGURE 2.49. D2 receptor blockade in the nigrostriatal pathway results in EPS. Unlike conventional antipsychotics, DA partial agonists do not completely remove the DA tone in this pathway, thus maintaining normal motor functioning and largely preventing the establishment of EPS.

Effects of D2 Partial Agonism on DA Circuitry: Part 1

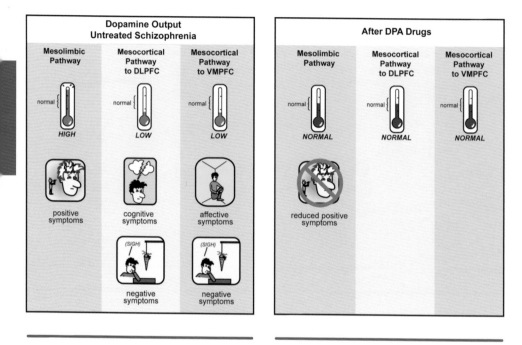

FIGURE 2.50. In untreated schizophrenia, DA output is high in the mesolimbic pathway, leading to positive symptoms, and low in the mesocortical pathways, leading to negative symptoms (projections to both DLPFC and VMPFC), cognitive symptoms (specifically the projections to the DLPFC), and affective symptoms (especially the projections to the VMPFC).

FIGURE 2.51. Administration of a DA partial agonist results in decreased DA output compared to the ultimate agonist, DA. Decreasing DA output in the mesolimbic DA pathway decreases the positive symptoms of psychosis, without affecting the experience of pleasure or reward. In the mesocortical pathways, where DA output is already low in schizophrenia, DA partial agonists may actually increase DA levels, thus improving the cognitive, negative, or affective symptoms of schizophrenia.

Effects of D2 Partial Agonism on DA Circuitry: Part 2

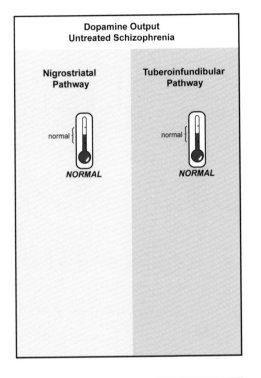

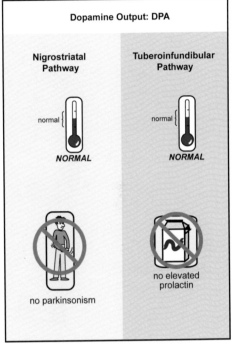

FIGURE 2.52. Unlike what is hypothesized for the mesolimbic and mesocortical pathways, DA output is theoretically normal in the nigrostriatal and tuberoinfundibular pathways. Thus it would make sense that one would not want to alter the normal activity in these pathways when treating schizophrenia.

FIGURE 2.53. In the nigrostriatal and tuberoinfundibular pathways, DA partial agonists should not drastically change DA output. Thus they would not lead to EPS and elevated prolactin levels.

Additional Receptors
Importance of D3 Receptors and Tonic Firing

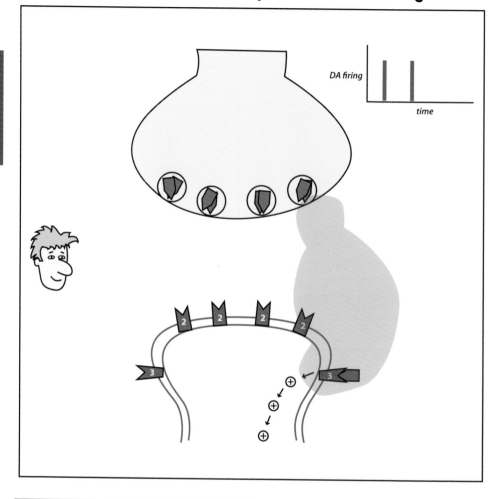

FIGURE 2.54. The role of dopamine D3 receptors is becoming increasingly important, as we learn more about their neurobiology, and as a large number of antipsychotics have effects at D3 receptors. Dopamine D3 receptors are located perisynaptically, meaning dopamine has to travel further outside the synapse to stimulate them. Modest levels of dopamine will first stimulate D3 receptors as these are more sensitive to dopamine than D1/2 receptors. Under normal conditions, stimulation of D3 receptors leads to tonic neuronal firing, theoretically allowing a person to feel content and happy.

Importance of D3 Receptors and Phasic Firing

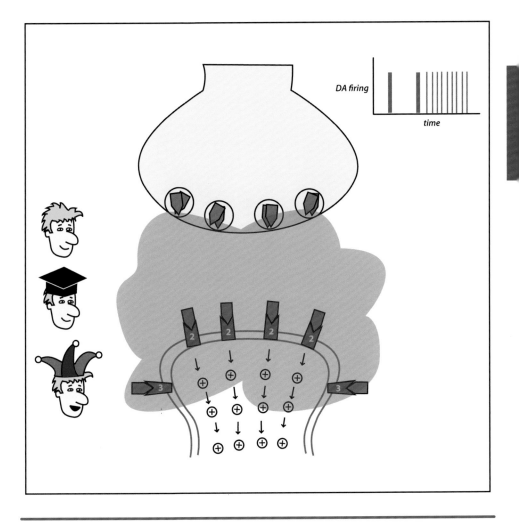

FIGURE 2.55. While tonic firing is often preferred in neuronal systems, a little bit of phasic firing of dopamine neurons can be a good thing. Phasic firing in the nucleus accumbens will lead to bursts of dopamine release and when this happens in a controlled manner it can reinforce learning and reward conditioning, which theoretically provides the motivation to pursue naturally rewarding experiences such as education, recognition, career development, enriching social and family connections, etc.

In the Absence of Tonic Firing

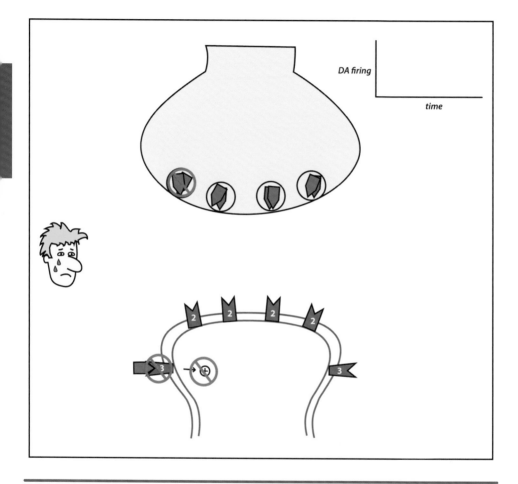

FIGURE 2.56. Hypothetically, in the absence of proper tonic firing via the dopamine D3 receptors, a person may start experiencing feelings of depression and the lack of wanting to participate in any pleasant activity.

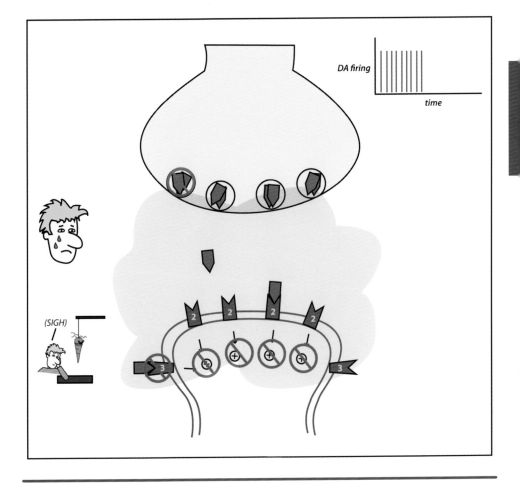

FIGURE 2.57. Tonic dopamine has the ability to modulate spiking phasic dopamine release. However, in the absence of tonic firing, phasic dopamine firing could be impaired, hypothetically resulting in the appearance of negative symptoms on top of the depression and anhedonia.

Treatment of Depression and Anhedonia

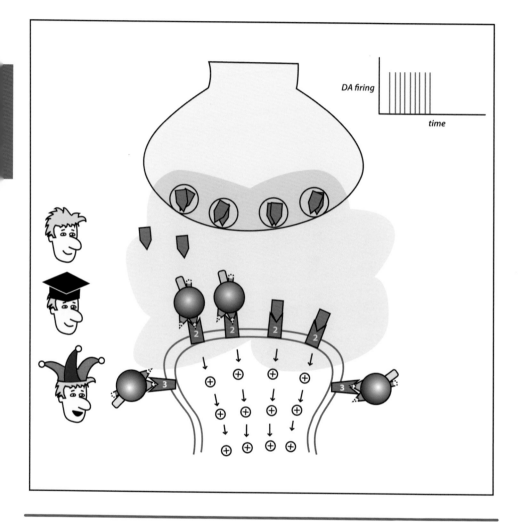

FIGURE 2.58. It is hypothetically possible to use a medication with D2/D3 partial agonist properties to treat the depression and anhedonia. The D3 partial agonist action will potentially reverse the depression, and lead to low levels of tonic firing, while partial stimulation of D2 receptors will allow for the reestablishment of low levels of phasic dopaminergic activity, thus treating the anhedonia. In this case the D2/D3 partial agonist acts as a net agonist. The patient may therefore feel cheerful again, and may want to engage in pleasurable activities.

In the Presence of Excessive Phasic Firing

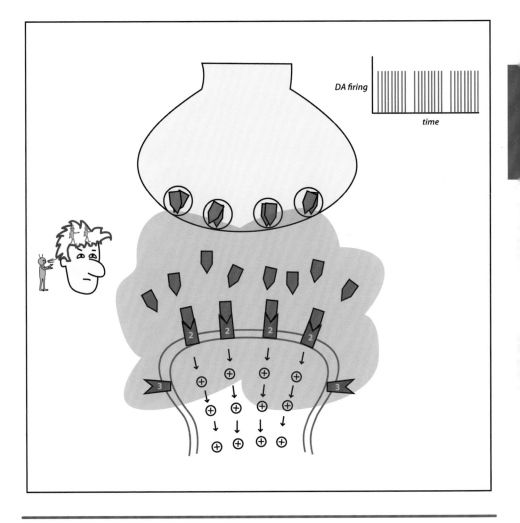

FIGURE 2.59. Excessive dopamine release can hypothetically lead to excessive phasic firing, and excessive stimulation of postsynaptic D2 receptors. As introduced in chapter 1, an overactive dopamine system may lead to the positive symptoms of schizophrenia.

Treatment of Positive Symptoms of Schizophrenia

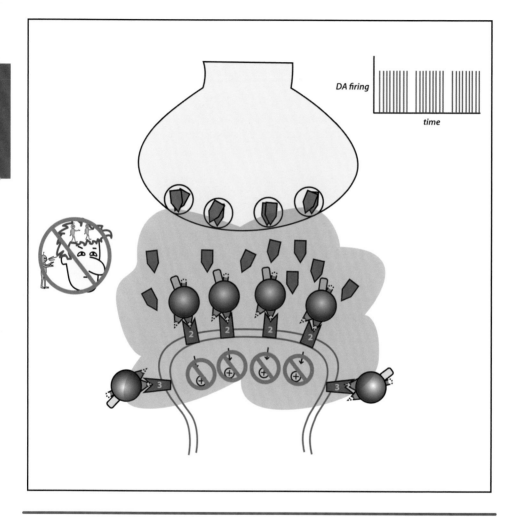

FIGURE 2.60. Medications with D2/D3 partial agonist properties can in this case act as a net antagonist, and block some of the excessive dopamine neurotransmission, thus resolving the positive symptoms of schizophrenia.

Relevance of NET, 5HT1A, and 5HT2C Receptors

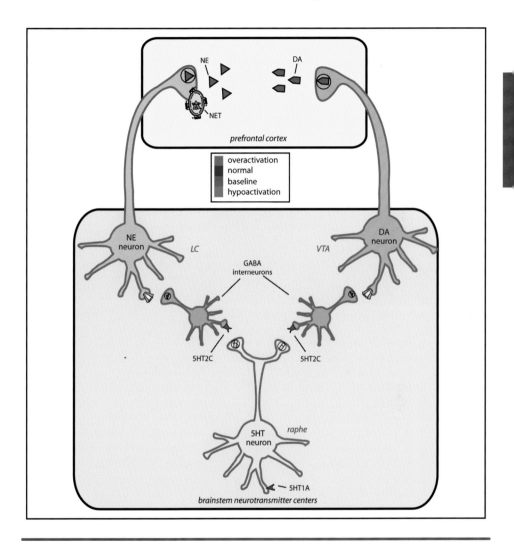

FIGURE 2.61. As mentioned earlier in chapter 1, the interactions between the serotonergic, norepinephrine, and dopaminergic pathways are of great importance in how antipsychotics lead to their clinical effects. The following few figures will exemplify what happens to norepinephrine and dopamine release (on top in prefrontal cortex) when the norepinephrine transporter, 5HT1A somatodendritc receptors (yellow neuron on the bottom), and/or 5HT2C receptors (located on dendrites of GABAergic interneurons) are modulated by endogenous molecules or by different medications.

Norepinephrine Transporters and Dopamine

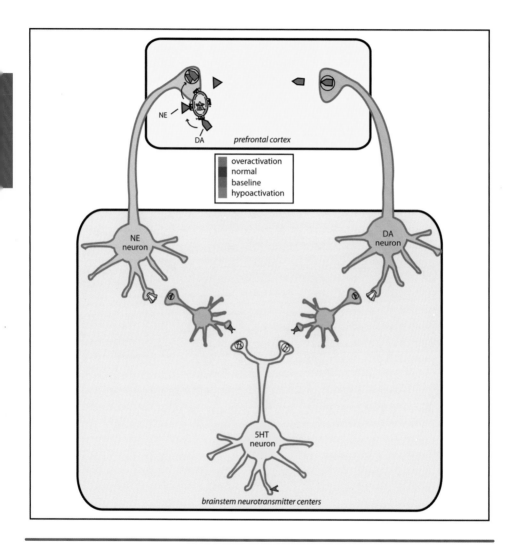

FIGURE 2.62. Unlike the abundance of norepinephrine transporters (NET), there are few dopamine transporters (DAT) in the prefrontal cortex, meaning that the released dopamine can diffuse away from the synapse and exert its actions further away. Dopamine can be removed from the synapse by reuptake via NET. Dopamine actually has a higher affinity for NET than norepinephrine, thus NET can modulate both norepinephrine and dopamine levels in the prefrontal cortex.

Effects of NET Inhibition on Norepinephrine and Dopamine

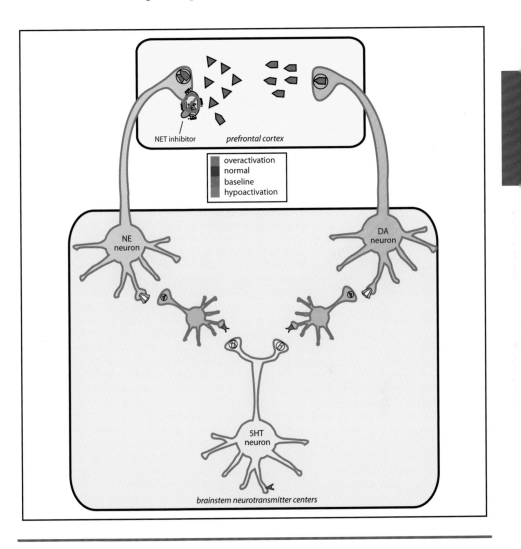

FIGURE 2.63. Blocking the norepinephrine transporter (NET) in the prefrontal cortex via a NET inhibitor will thus result in increased norepinephrine and dopamine levels, as both neurotransmitters normally get removed from the synapse via this mechanism. The resulting increase in cortical neurotransmitter levels could be effective at treating mood and cognitive disorders.

Effects of 5HT1A Stimulation on Norepinephrine and Dopamine Cortical Neurons

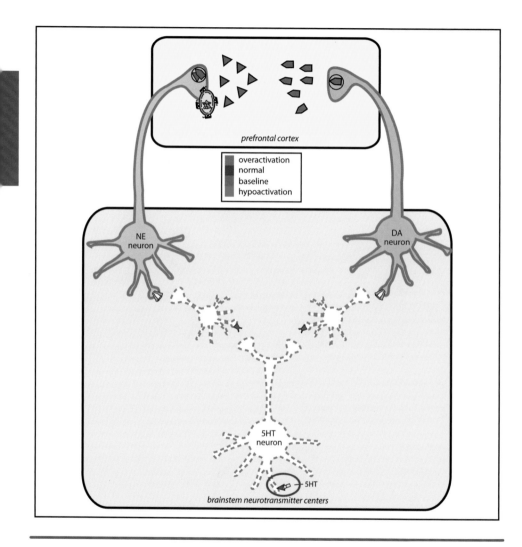

FIGURE 2.64. When serotonin, or a 5HT1A agonist, binds to 5HT1A receptors in the brainstem, this will lead to inhibition of the serotonergic neuron. The lack of serotonergic stimulation of GABAergic interneurons will result in inhibition of these interneurons. In the absence of the inhibitory tone from GABAergic interneurons, norepinephrine and dopamine neurons will become overactivated causing enhanced release of norepinephrine and dopamine in the prefrontal cortex, which could possible be effective at treating mood and cognitive disorders.

Effects of 5HT2C Stimulation on Norepinephrine and Dopamine Cortical Neurons

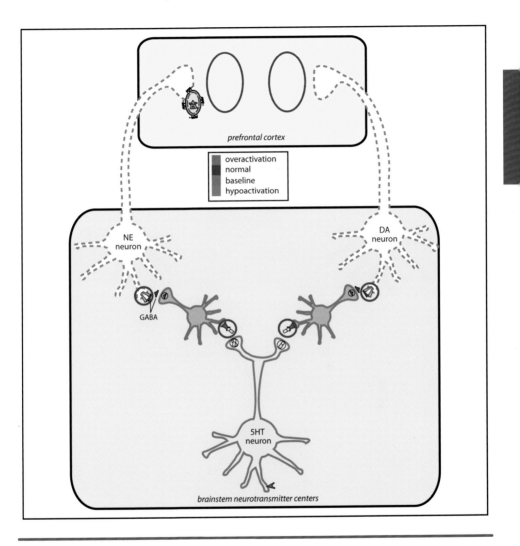

FIGURE 2.65. On the contrary to what occurs following 5HT1A receptor stimulation by serotonin, activating 5HT2C receptors on GABAergic interneurons will lead to increased inhibition of norepinephrine and dopamine neurons. This will result in the shut-down of norepinephrine and dopamine release in the prefrontal cortex.

Effects of 5HT2C Blockade on Norepinephrine and Dopamine Cortical Neurons

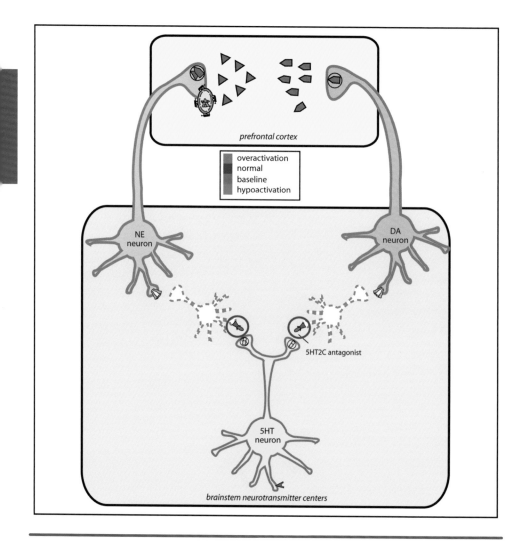

FIGURE 2.66. It is thus not surprising that blockade of 5HT2C receptors on GABA-ergic interneurons would lead to disinhibition of norepinephrine and dopamine neurons, resulting in increased release of cortical norepinephrine and dopamine levels, which could again be effective at treating mood and cognitive disorders.

Effects of Multifunctional Drugs

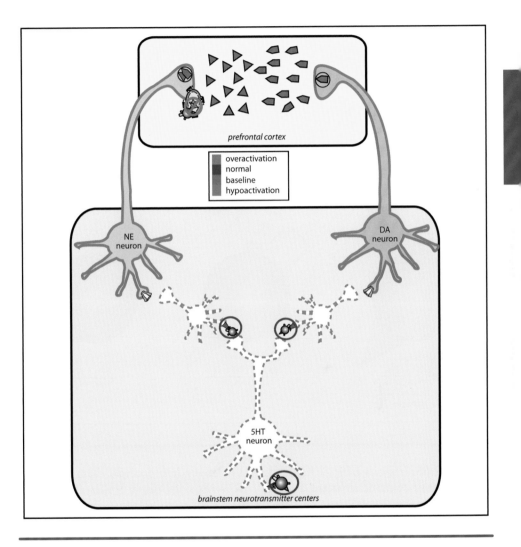

FIGURE 2.67. Multifunctional medications that encompass all of the properties mentioned in the previous figures, such as partial 5HT1A agonism, 5HT2C antagonism, and norepinephrine reuptake inhibition can work at different levels within this circuitry and may be effective at treating mood and cognitive disorders. The active metabolite of quetiapine, norquetiapine, as well as ziprasidone have all three of these properties.

5HT1A Partial Agonism (SPA) of Atypical Antipsychotics

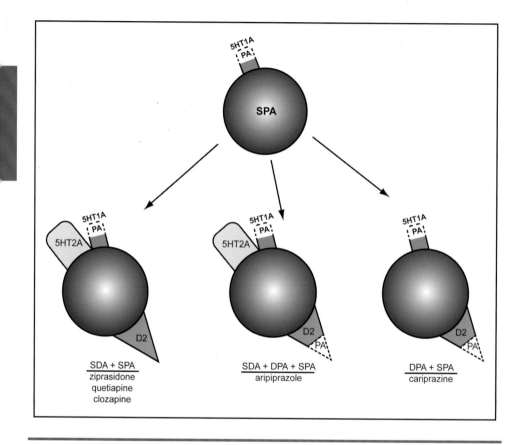

FIGURE 2.68. Various antipsychotics do not fit neatly into a single class of drugs because they combine different receptor actions. Besides being 5HT2A/D2 blockers, ziprasidone, quetiapine, and clozapine are also partial agonists at 5HT1A receptors.

The D2 partial agonist aripiprazole is also an antagonist at 5HT2A receptors and a partial agonist at 5HT1A receptors. Besides being a D2 partial agonist, cariprazine is also a partial agonist at the 5HT1A receptor.

Atypical Antipsychotics with 5HT2C Properties

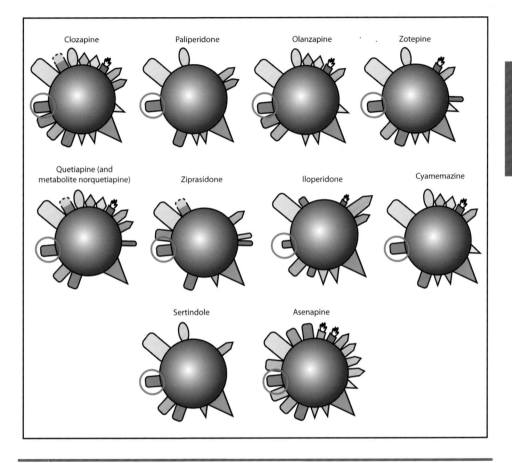

FIGURE 2.69. Atypical antipsychotics have many different properties which can be beneficial in different patients. The medications shown above all have 5HT2C blocking properties.

Atypical Antipsychotics with NET Properties

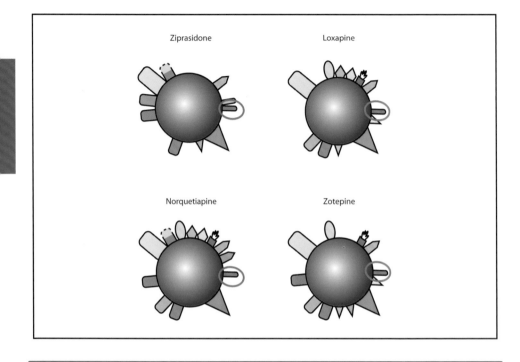

FIGURE 2.70. Atypical antipsychotics have many different properties which can be beneficial in different patients. The medications shown above all have NET blocking properties.

5HT7: The New Receptor of Interest

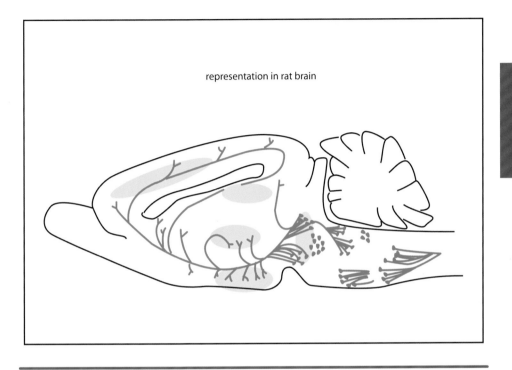

representation in rat brain

FIGURE 2.71. The 5HT7 receptor has gained attention as many atypical antipsychotics (such as clozapine, amisulpride, risperidone, paliperidone, quetiapine, ziprasidone, zotepine, sertindole, loxapine, cyamemazine, iloperidone, asenapine) exhibit variable affinity for this receptor. The novel antipsychotic lurasidone, in late stage clinical development, has the most potent 5HT7 antagonist properties among all of its receptor binding actions. While the exact role in the reduction of psychotic symptoms of 5HT7 receptors is still under investigation it appears to be an important receptor due to its localization throughout the brain. 5HT7 receptors are involved in mood and sleep (cortex), in learning and memory, in stress (hippocampus), in sleep and epilepsy (thalamus), in circadian rhythm, thermoregulation, and endocrine regulation (hypothalamus), and in circadian rhythm and mood (raphe).

Side Effects of Antipsychotics: Metabolic Issues and Sedation

This chapter will go over the metabolic issues and other side effects associated with the different classes of antipsychotics, and explain how an informed psychopharmacologist can ascertain that side effects are minimized and optimal treatment is maximized. Whereas Chapter 4 will expand upon the effects that antipsychotics have on the brain—or the pharmacodynamics of antipsychotics—this chapter includes a section that explains the pharmacokinetics of antipsychotics, namely how brain and body interactions affect the drugs. These are important concepts to understand in order to maximize treatment and minimize side effects.

Which Receptors Can Hypothetically Lead to Cardiometabolic Risk?

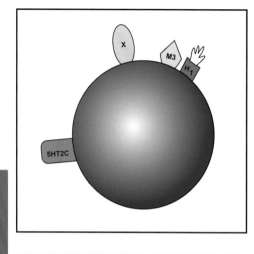

FIGURE 3.1. There are a few receptors that, hypothetically, might increase cardiometabolic risk; these include 5HT2C, M3, and H1 receptors, as well as receptors yet to be identified (signified here as receptor "X").

Specifically, 5HT2C and H1 antagonism is linked to weight gain, and M3 receptor antagonism can alter insulin regulation. Receptor "X" may increase insulin resistance, resulting in elevated fasting plasma triglyceride levels. Some patients might be more prone than others to experience increased cardiometabolic risk on certain atypical antipsychotics.

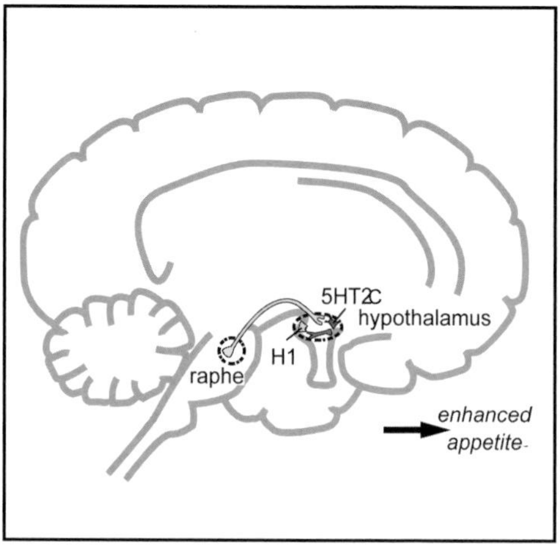

FIGURE 3.2. Simultaneous blockade of 5HT2C and H1 receptors can lead to weight gain, which could result from increased appetite stimulation via hypothalamic eating centers.

Weight Gain and Cardiometabolic Risk of Antipsychotics

Antipsychotic	Weight Gain Risk
Clozapine	+++
Olanzapine	+++
Risperidone*	++
Quetiapine	++
Ziprasidone	+/-
Aripiprazole	+/-

* Paliperidone (active metabolite of risperidone) carries the same weight gain risk.
+++ high risk
++ intermediate risk
+/- low risk

Antipsychotic	Cardiometabolic Risk
Ziprasidone	Low
Aripiprazole	Low
Amisulpride	Possibly low, not well studied
Iloperidone	Possibly low, currently studied
Asenapine	Possibly low, currently studied

TABLE 3.1. Various atypical antipsychotics and their risk of weight gain. The information reflects FDA and expert agreement on three tiers of risk based on data in adults. Antipsychotic-induced weight gain in children and adolescents is not as well studied; however, there is preliminary evidence to suggest not only that youths also experience antipsychotic-induced weight gain, but that this may occur even with agents considered weight neutral in adults.

TABLE 3.2. Some atypical antipsychotics are "metabolically friendly," in that they are low-risk for both weight gain and cardiometabolic illness.

The Metabolic Highway

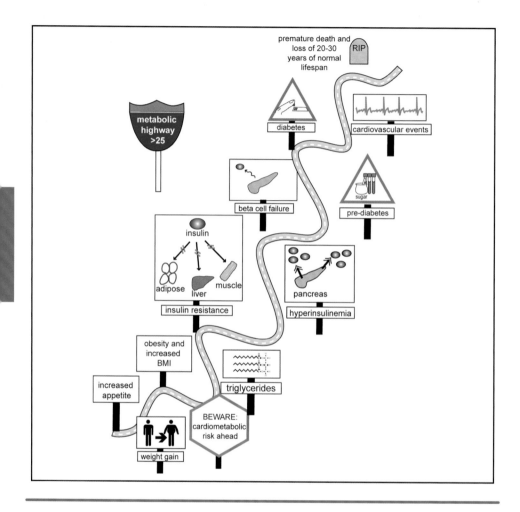

FIGURE 3.3. The metabolic highway depicts different stages that precede cardiovascular disease and premature death. Increased appetite and weight gain combined with a body mass index greater than 25 is the "entrance ramp" to the highway. The highway will eventually lead down the following path: obesity, insulin resistance, and dyslipidemia with increased fasting triglyceride levels.

When hyperinsulinemia leads to pancreatic beta cell failure, pre-diabetes and then diabetes ensue. The presence of diabetes increases a patient's risk for cardiovascular events and premature death.

Insulin Resistance and Antipsychotics

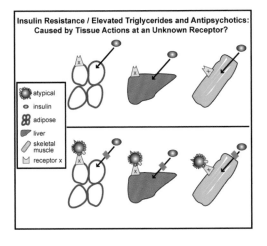

Insulin Resistance / Elevated Triglycerides and Antipsychotics: Caused by Tissue Actions at an Unknown Receptor?

atypical
insulin
adipose
liver
skeletal muscle
receptor x

Blocking M3 Cholinergic Receptors: Reduces Insulin Release

presynaptic parasympathetic fibers

postsynaptic cholinergic fibers

beta cells

pancreas

ACh
M3
insulin

SDA
insulin

FIGURE 3.4. An unknown pharmacological mechanism is most likely responsible for increased insulin resistance and elevated fasting triglycerides, as seen following the administration of some atypical antipsychotics. In this figure a hypothetical "receptor X" could be the mediator of these actions, allowing atypical antipsychotics to bind to it and leading to insulin resistance of adipose tissue, liver, and skeletal muscle.

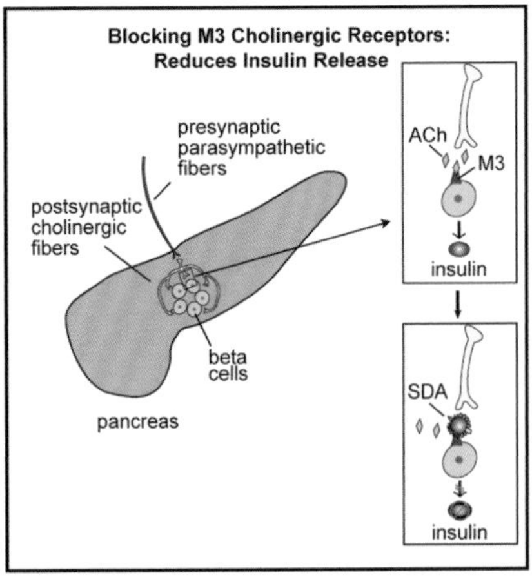

FIGURE 3.5. Atypical antipsychotics can in rare cases lead to diabetic ketoacidosis (DKA). Normally, insulin secretion is regulated by parasympathetic cholinergic neurons innervating the pancreas and stimulating M3 receptors on pancreatic beta cells. Thus if an atypical antipsychotic has antimuscarinic properties at the M3 receptor, it could potentially lead to reduced insulin release. This could be problematic in patients requiring the cholinergic pathway for the regulation of insulin secretion.

Where on the Metabolic Highway Should Antipsychotic Treatment Be Monitored?

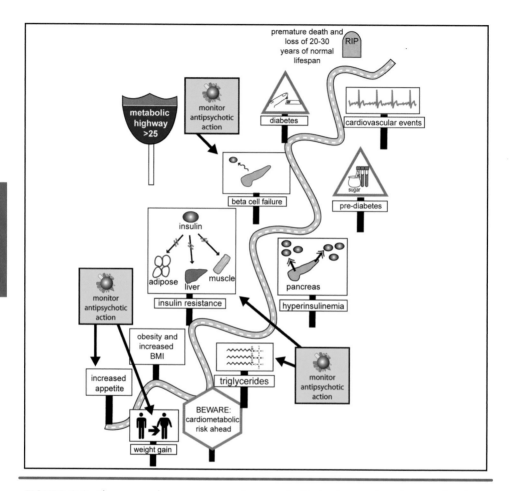

FIGURE 3.6. There are three spots on the metabolic highway that the psychopharmacologist can use to determine whether a patient is "speeding" toward increased cardiometabolic risk when taking different antipsychotics. First, weight gain and body mass index need to be monitored, as both could suggest an increase in appetite and could lead to obesity. Second, fasting triglyceride levels need to be monitored to determine whether the atypical antipsychotic is leading to insulin resistance. Third, it is imperative to educate patients about the symptoms of diabetic ketoacidosis and hyperglycemic hyperosmolar syndrome and to measure fasting glucose levels, as atypical antipsychotics can induce those symptoms suddenly. Although formal monitoring guidelines only exist for adults, youths not only should be monitored but may even need to be monitored more frequently than adutls.

Monitoring and Managing Antipsychotics: Best Practices

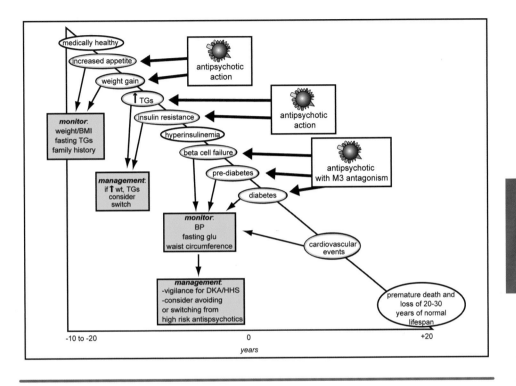

FIGURE 3.7. What are the best practices for monitoring and managing antipsychotics? Patients who will be dosed with atypical antipsychotics should undergo baseline measurements including weight, body mass index (BMI), and fasting triglyceride levels (TGs), and they should provide a family history of diabetes. Weight, BMI, and fasting triglycerides should be monitored throughout treatment, and if weight or triglyceride levels increase, then the patient should be switched to a different antipsychotic, have therapeutic lifestyle interventions, or both.

When patients have dyslipidemia, are pre-diabetic or diabetic, or are obese, it is necessary to obtain their fasting glucose levels, blood pressure, and waist circumference measurements just before starting treatment with antipsychotics and throughout treatment. It may be best in these patients to avoid or switch from antipsychotics that exhibit a higher risk of cardiometabolic side effects.

The Involvement of a Psychopharmacologist

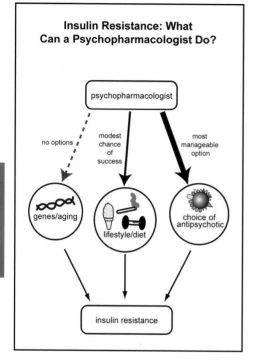

Insulin Resistance: What Can a Psychopharmacologist Do?

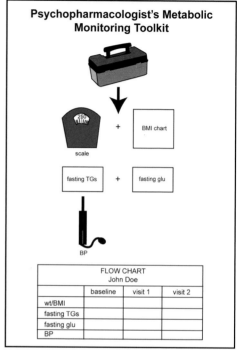

Psychopharmacologist's Metabolic Monitoring Toolkit

FIGURE 3.8. Although a psychopharmacologist can individualize the choice of an atypical antipsychotic, there are various factors that are out of his/her control. These include genetic factors such as age, family history, etc. The psychopharmacologist can also put power into the patients' hands by educating them on lifestyle choices, such as diet, exercise, and smoking. However, the most manageable option for cardiometabolic risk may be which antipsychotic the patient takes.

FIGURE 3.9. A simple metabolic toolkit can be used to track the four main parameters: weight/BMI, fasting triglycerides, fasting glucose, and blood pressure. By recording those items at the beginning of treatment and getting regular laboratory tests done for fasting triglycerides and fasting glucose, it is possible to simply monitor a patient and prevent the occurrence of future devastating side effects.

Sedation and Antipsychotics

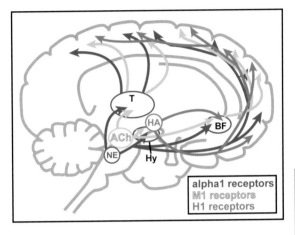

alpha1 receptors
M1 receptors
H1 receptors

FIGURE 3.10. D2, M1, H1, and alpha1 adrenergic receptor antagonism can all lead to sedation. Thus the atypical antipsychotics with those receptor properties will at some level or another alter arousal in patients.

FIGURE 3.11. Acetylcholine (ACh), histamine (HA), and norepinephrine (NE) are all involved in arousal pathways, thereby connecting neurotransmitter centers with the thalamus (T), hypothalamus (Hy), basal forebrain (BF), and cortex. Thus, it is predictable that atypical antipsychotics with pharmacologic actions that block these receptors could be associated with sedating effects.

Sedation as a Therapeutic Tool

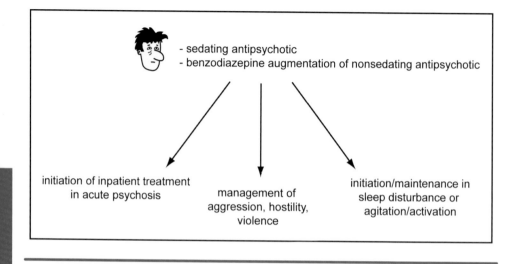

- sedating antipsychotic
- benzodiazepine augmentation of nonsedating antipsychotic

initiation of inpatient treatment in acute psychosis

management of aggression, hostility, violence

initiation/maintenance in sleep disturbance or agitation/activation

FIGURE 3.12. Although it is preferable to avoid long-term sedation, it can be useful initially in the treatment of schizophrenia. Short-term sedation can aid in managing acute psychosis, aggression, hostility, violence, sleep disturbances, or agitation/activation. A sedating antipsychotic or an adjunct benzodiazepine can be used to induce sedation.

The Reasons for Noncompliance to Antipsychotics

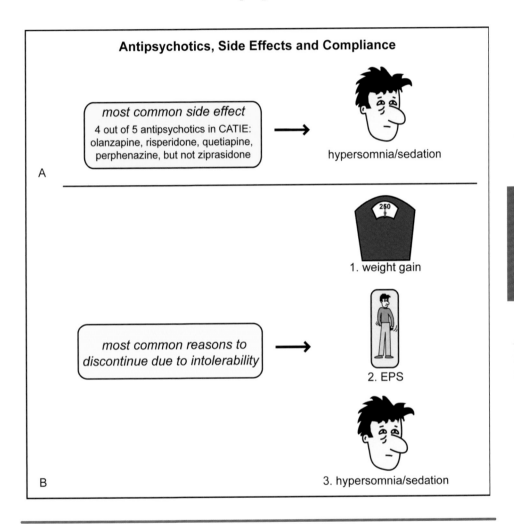

Antipsychotics, Side Effects and Compliance

A

most common side effect

4 out of 5 antipsychotics in CATIE: olanzapine, risperidone, quetiapine, perphenazine, but not ziprasidone

→ hypersomnia/sedation

B

most common reasons to discontinue due to intolerability

→

1. weight gain

2. EPS

3. hypersomnia/sedation

FIGURE 3.13. (A) The most common side effect of atypical antipsychotics is sedation, as seen in four of the five antipsychotics studied in the CATIE trial (Clinical Antipsychotic Trials of Intervention Effectiveness).

(B) Although short-term sedation can be beneficial, long-term sedation should be avoided. It is among the top three reasons for discontinuing antipsychotic treatment due to intolerability, after weight gain and EPS.

How Can Functional Outcome Be Optimized?

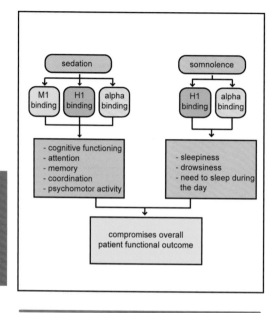

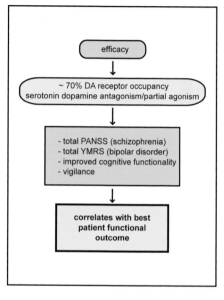

FIGURE 3.14. Blockade of muscarinic M1, histamine H1, and/or alpha1 adrenergic receptors can lead to sedation, which can impact cognitive functioning, attention, memory, and coordination. All of these will result in poor overall functioning for patients with schizophrenia. Somnolence, which can lead to sleepiness and drowsiness, is most likely mediated by blockade of H1 and alpha1 adrenergic receptors. These symptoms can also affect the overall functioning of the patient.

FIGURE 3.15. An adequate treatment of schizophrenia aims to resolve positive symptoms, as well as affective, cognitive, and negative symptoms. Pharmacologically, this requires approximately 70% blockade of D2 receptors in the nucleus accumbens, in addition to antagonism/partial agonism of D2, 5HT2A, and 5HT1A receptors in other key brain regions. Antagonism of histamine H1, muscarinic M1, or alpha 1 adrenergic receptors is best avoided, as these lead to most of the side effects seen with antipsychotics.

The Pathway to Efficacy

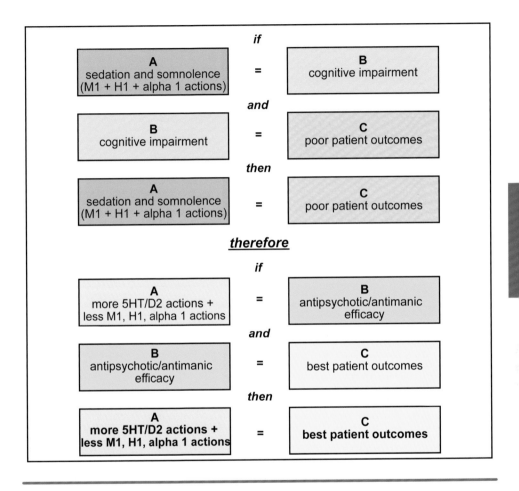

FIGURE 3.16. In order to reach efficacy in the treatment of schizophrenia it is important to ascertain the best possible patient outcome. If blockade of M1, H1, and alpha1 receptors causes sedation and somnolence (which are associated with cognitive impairment), then using antipsychotics with those properties would be related to poor patient outcomes.

If, on the other hand, blockade of 5HT and DA receptors has antimanic and antipsychotic efficacy, thus leading to good patient outcome, it would be best to use an antipsychotic that has a 5HT/DA profile, but lacks efficacy at M1, H1, or alpha 1 receptors.

How to Reach the Best Long-Term Outcomes in Schizophrenia?

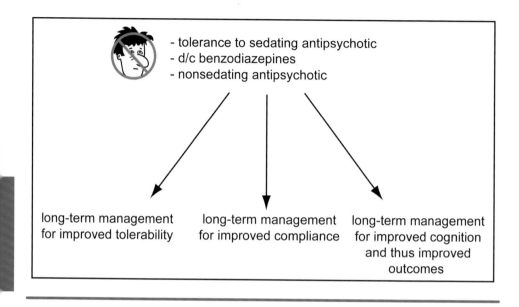

- tolerance to sedating antipsychotic
- d/c benzodiazepines
- nonsedating antipsychotic

long-term management for improved tolerability

long-term management for improved compliance

long-term management for improved cognition and thus improved outcomes

FIGURE 3.17. As one of the top reasons for discontinuing an antipsychotic for intolerability, long-term sedation is best avoided. Patients whose nonsedating antipsychotic medication was initially augmented with a benzodiazepine may need to discontinue the benzodiazepine. For some patients treated with a sedating antipsychotic, it might be necessary to change their medication.

Other patients might become tolerant to the sedating side effects of their medication. Careful monitoring to develop individualized treatment is necessary in determining the best possible treatment plan for each patient.

Enzymatic Metabolism of a Drug: The Cytochrome P450 System

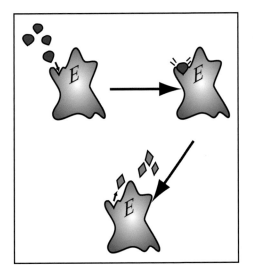

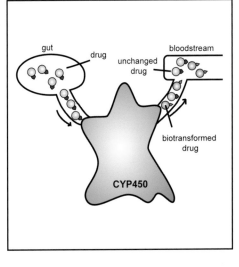

FIGURE 3.18. After a substrate binds to the active site on the enzyme, it is converted into a product which is then released from the enzyme. Some drugs are inhibitors of enzymes; they can either be reversible or irreversible inhibitors. The reversible inhibitor will allow a substrate to compete for the binding site; thus the substrate can reverse the inhibition of the enzyme. In the case of irreversible inhibitors, the substrate cannot displace the inhibitor, and the enzyme essentially becomes unusable. In this case, enzymatic activity is only restored when a new enzyme molecule is synthesized by the cell's DNA.

FIGURE 3.19. The cytochrome P450 (CYP450) enzyme system, which is located in the gut wall and liver, is responsible for the way the body metabolizes drugs such as antipsychotics. When the drug substrate passes through the gut, it is biotransformed into a product released into the bloodstream. Thus upon administration, a drug is partially metabolized by the CYP450 system and partially left unchanged.

Specifics of the CYP450 System

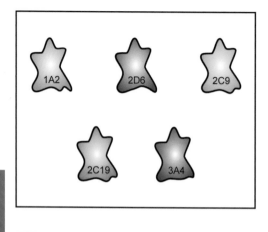

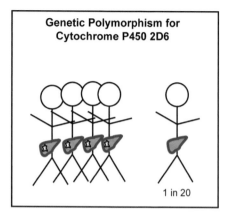

Genetic Polymorphism for Cytochrome P450 2D6

1 in 20

FIGURE 3.20. The cytochrome P450 system encompasses a large number of enzymes. These are classified according to family, subtype, and gene product, using the following nomenclature: 1=family, A=subtype, and 1=gene product. Thus, as depicted in the figure, the five most common and relevant systems are CYP450 1A2, 2D6, 2C9, 2C19, and 3A4.

FIGURE 3.21. Risperidone, clozapine, olanzapine, and aripiprazole are all substrates for the cytochrome P450 2D6 enzyme. An individual's genetic make-up determines which CYP450 enzymes s/he has. For example, approximately 1 in 20 Caucasians is a poor metabolizer via 2D6 and thus needs to metabolize drugs by an alternative route. This may (1) not be as metabolically efficient and (2) explain the differential efficacy of various antipsychotics in different patients.

Metabolism of Antipsychotics by CYP450 Enzymes

Drug	Metabolized by
Clozapine	CYP450 1A2, 3A4, 2D6
Risperidone	CYP450 2D6
Paliperidone	Is only weakly metabolized
Olanzapine	CYP450 1A2
Quetiapine	CYP450 3A4, 2D6
Ziprasidone	Not affected by CYP450 enzymes
Aripiprazole	CYP450 3A4, 2D6
Zotepine	CYP450 1A2, 3A4
Perospirone	CYP450 3A4
Sertindole	CYP450 3A4, 2D6
Loxapine	Unknown
Cyamemazine	Unknown
Amisulpride	Is only weakly metabolized
Sulpiride	Is only weakly metabolized
Bifeprunox	CYP450 2C9, 3A4, only little 2D6
Iloperidone	CYP450 3A4, 2D6
Asenapine	CYP450 1A2, 3A4

TABLE 3.3. The hepatic enzymes involved in the metabolism of the 17 antipsychotics described in Chapter 4.

Importance of the CYP450 1A2 Enzyme

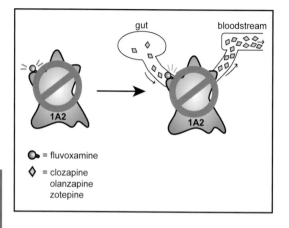

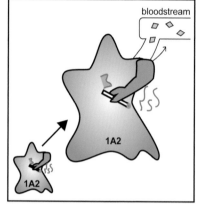

FIGURE 3.22. As different drug classes are substrates for different CYP450 enzymes, it is important to understand drug interactions. The antipsychotics clozapine, olanzapine, and zotepine are substrates for cytochrome P450 1A2. If these are given in combination with an antidepressant such as fluvoxamine, which acts as an inhibitor of this enzyme, plasma levels can rise. Thus it is important to know which drugs a patient is taking and to be prepared for the need to adjust dosages.

FIGURE 3.23. Patients with schizophrenia are known to self-medicate by smoking cigarettes. Smoking can induce the enzyme cytochrome P450 1A2, so that the plasma levels of drugs metabolized by this enzyme such as olanzapine, clozapine, and zotepine are lowered. Smokers may therefore need higher levels of these three drugs compared to non-smokers.

Importance of the CYP450 2D6 Enzyme

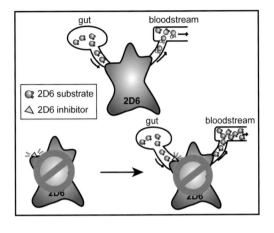

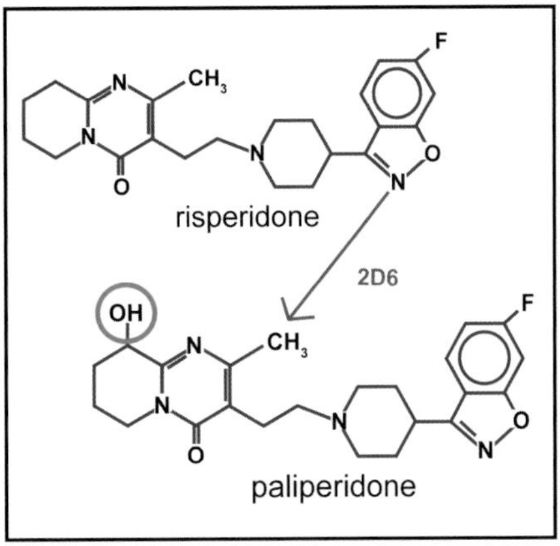

FIGURE 3.24. Risperidone, clozapine, olanzapine, and aripiprazole are substrates for the cytochrome P450 2D6 enzyme. This enzyme often hydroxylates its substrates.

Various antidepressants such as paroxetine, fluoxetine, duloxetine, and high doses of sertraline are inhibitors of cytochrome P450 2D6; thus they could theoretically raise the levels of the previously mentioned antipsychotics as these are substrates for the same enzyme. However, this is not usually clinically significant.

FIGURE 3.25. Risperidone is metabolized to paliperidone by the enzyme cytochrome P450 2D6. This active metabolite has been approved as a new antipsychotic.

Importance of the CYP450 3A4 Enzyme

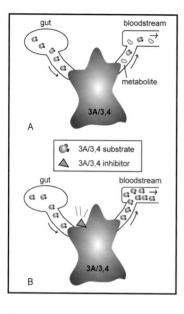

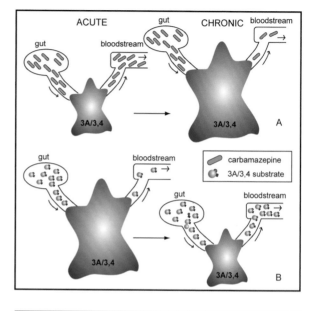

FIGURE 3.26. (A) Clozapine, quetiapine, ziprasidone, sertindole, aripiprazole, and zotepine are substrates for cytochrome P450 3A4. (B) Powerful inhibitors of cytochrome P450 3A4 include the antifungal ketoconazole, some protease inhibitors, the antibiotic erythromycin, and the following antidepressants: fluvoxamine, nefazodone, fluoxetine, and its metabolite norfluoxetine. In the presence of these inhibitors, plasma levels of antipsychotics will be elevated, and thus might need to be adjusted.

FIGURE 3.27. (A) Besides being a substrate or an inhibitor of a cytochrome P450 enzyme, drugs can also be inducers of the system. The mood stabilizer carbamazepine is one such example. The presence of carbamazepine increases the metabolism of the substrates of the 3A4 enzyme, thus requiring higher doses of the substrates. (B) At the same time, if a patient who was taking, for example, carbamazepine in combination with clozapine (a substrate for 3A4) was discontinuing the mood stabilizer, it would be necessary to adjust the dose of the antipsychotic as well. As the autoinduction of 3A4 by carbamazepine would be reversed over time, the original dose of an antipsychotic would be too high.

Individual Antipsychotic Drugs

This chapter will describe each antipsychotic medication currently available in terms of side effect profile, dosing tips, and drug interactions. As with all atypical antipsychotics discussed in this chapter, binding properties vary greatly with technique and from one laboratory to another; they are constantly being revised and updated. Thus it is important to remain up-to-date on the specifics of each antipsychotic. This chapter will also introduce some of the new medications that are in development.

Symbols Used in this Chapter			
	Life-threatening or dangerous side effects		Drug Interactions
	Tips and Pearls		Cardiac Impairment
	Children and Adolescents		Renal Impairment
	Pregnancy		Hepatic Impairment

Clozapine

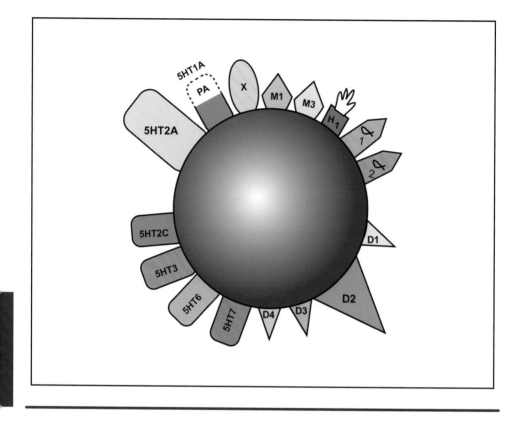

FIGURE 4.1. The most complex receptor profile belongs to clozapine. It has been considered the "prototypical" atypical antipsychotic and leads to few EPS, does not result in tardive dyskinesia and does not elevate prolactin levels. It has proven particularly efficacious when other antipsychotics fail.

Even though it is very effective, clozapine is not considered a first-line agent as it can lead to the potentially life-threatening side effect agranulocytosis. Weight increase and the concomitant risk of developing metabolic complications are greatest with clozapine.

Clozapine: Tips and Pearls

 Dosing

Formulation:
12.5, 25, 50, and 100 mg tablets;
12.5, 25, 50, and 100 mg orally disintegrating tablets

Dosage Range:
300–450 mg/day

Approved For:
Treatment-resistant schizophrenia; reduction in risk of recurrent suicidal behavior in patients with schizophrenia or schizoaffective disorder

Pearls

 Rapid discontinuation can lead to rebound psychosis; most efficacious but most dangerous; reduces suicide in schizophrenia

Potentially efficacious in early-onset treatment-resistant schizophrenia; children and adolescents should be monitored more often than adults

Pregnancy risk category B (animal studies do not show adverse effects, no controlled studies in humans)

Side effects I

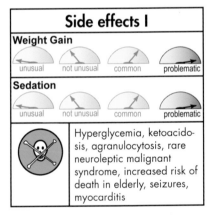

Weight Gain

unusual — not unusual — common — problematic

Sedation

unusual — not unusual — common — problematic

Hyperglycemia, ketoacidosis, agranulocytosis, rare neuroleptic malignant syndrome, increased risk of death in elderly, seizures, myocarditis

Side effects II

 CYP450 1A2, 3A4, and 2D6 inhibitors increase its plasma levels; CYP450 1A2 inducers decrease its levels; drug enhances effects of antihypertensives

Use with caution, especially if patient takes concomitant medications

Use with caution in patients with renal impairments

Use with caution in patients with hepatic impairments

FIGURE 4.2. Dosing and interaction information for clozapine.

Risperidone

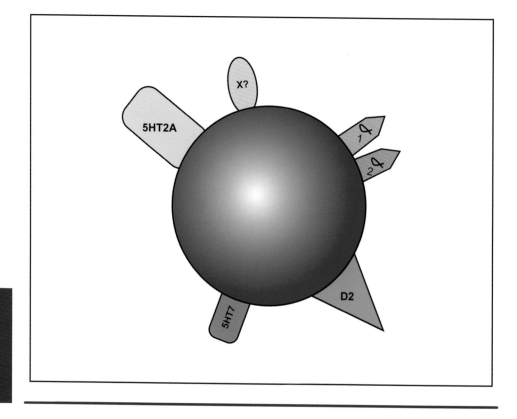

FIGURE 4.3. The receptor profile for risperidone is certainly simpler than the one for clozapine. Risperidone is mostly a 5HT2A/D2 antagonist. At low doses risperidone behaves like an atypical antipsychotic, but if the doses are pushed it can, similarly to conventional drugs, lead to EPS. The long-acting intramuscular (IM) formulation of risperidone has been approved for bipolar maintenance, either as monotherapy or as adjunct to lithium or valproate. Risperidone is approved for use in children and adolescents for the following disorders: irritability associated with autistic disorder (ages 5 to 16), bipolar disorder (ages 10 to 17), and schizophrenia (ages 13 to 17).

Risperidone is also available as an intramuscular, long-term depot formulation that lasts two weeks. Risperidone does increase prolactin levels, but there appears to be less risk of weight gain with risperidone, as well as less cardiometabolic risk, than with some other atypical antipsychotics, at least in some patients.

Risperidone: Tips and Pearls

 Dosing

Formulation:
0.25, 0.5, 1, 2, 3, 4, and 6 mg tablets; 0.5, 1, and 2 mg orally disintegrating tablets; 1mg/mL liquid; 25, 37.5 and 50 mg vial/kit IM depot

Dosage Range:
2–8 mg/day oral (psychosis); 0.5–2 mg/day oral (children and elderly); 25–50 mg depot every 2 weeks

Approved For:
Schizophrenia, delaying relapse in schizophrenia, other psychotic disorders, acute mania/mixed mania, bipolar maintenance (IM formulation)

Side effects I

Weight Gain

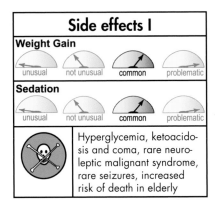

unusual | not unusual | **common** | problematic

Sedation

unusual | not unusual | **common** | problematic

Hyperglycemia, ketoacidosis and coma, rare neuroleptic malignant syndrome, rare seizures, increased risk of death in elderly

Pearls

 Less may be more; good treatment for agitation (elderly) and behavioral symptoms (children); dose-dependent EPS; less weight gain and sedation than other drugs

 Approved for autism-related irritability (ages 5 to 16), bipolar (ages 10 to 17), schizophrenia (ages 13 to 17)

Pregnancy risk category C (some animal studies show adverse effects; no controlled studies in humans)

Side effects II

 CYP450 2D6 inhibitors can increase its plasma levels; drug increases effects of antihypertensives and decreases DA agonist effects

Use with caution in elderly with atrial fibrillation

In patients with renal impairments, only use long-acting depot if patient tolerates oral formulation

In patients with hepatic impairments, only use long-acting depot if patient tolerates oral formulation

FIGURE 4.4. Dosing and interaction information for risperidone.

Paliperidone

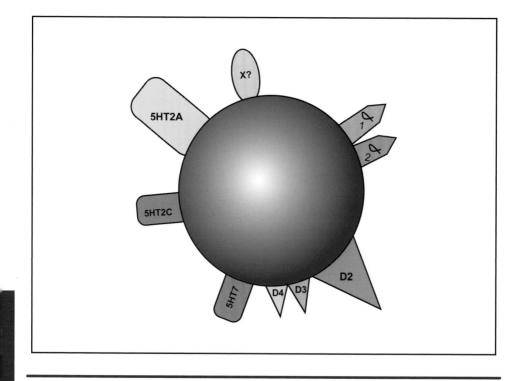

FIGURE 4.5. Paliperidone, also a 5HT2A/D2 antagonist, is the active metabolite of risperidone, and thus has a similar receptor profile. The oral sustained-release formulation of paliperidone allows it to be taken just once a day. In some patients, this property could lead to less EPS and sedation compared to its parent compound.

Paliperidone may theoretically improve depression due to its alpha 2 antagonist properties but has not been extensively studied. It might however be associated with weight gain, insulin resistance, and diabetes as well as prolactin elevation, similarly to risperidone.

Paliperidone is the first atypical antipsychotic that has recently been approved as a once-monthly formulation for the acute and maintenace treatment of schizophrenia in the United States.

Paliperidone: Tips and Pearls

 Dosing

Formulation:
1.5, 3, 6, and 9 mg extended-release tablets; prefilled syringes containing 39, 78, 117, 156, or 234 mg paliperidone palmitate (extended-release injectable suspension)

Dosage Range:
Recommended monthly dose for injectable is 117 mg, dosage range is 39 mg to 234 mg depending on individual; for extended-release tablets: 3–12 mg/day, with 6 mg/day having optimum efficacy; no titration required

Approved For:
Acute and maintenance treatment of schizophrenia, tablets also approved for acute treatment of schizoaffective disorder as monotherapy or as adjunct to mood stabilizer and/or antidepressant

Side effects I

Weight Gain

unusual | **not unusual** | common | problematic

Sedation

unusual | **not unusual** | common | problematic

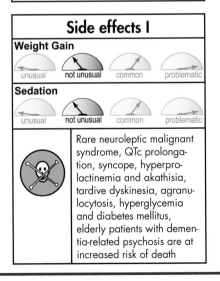 Rare neuroleptic malignant syndrome, QTc prolongation, syncope, hyperprolactinemia and akathisia, tardive dyskinesia, agranulocytosis, hyperglycemia and diabetes mellitus, elderly patients with dementia-related psychosis are at increased risk of death

Pearls

 Dose-dependent risk of EPS; may elevate prolactin levels and cause weight gain (especially at higher doses); beneficial for people with liver disease or for people on antidepressant (as no interaction with CYP450 enzyme); once-monthly formulation

 Preliminary study suggests efficacy in children and adolescents, however, safety in patients younger than age 18 has not been established

 Not recommended during pregnancy or breast feeding; insufficient data in humans

Side effects II

 Not metabolized by liver, thus low potential for interactions with other drugs; carbamazepine decreases and divalproex sodium increases the plasma levels of paliperidone requiring a dose adjustment of paliperidone

Use with caution in patients with cardiac impairments

Recommended initial dose for mild renal impairment is 3 mg/day, for moderate to severe renal impairment is 1.5 mg/day, not recommended in patients with severe renal impairment (creatinine clearance <10 mL/min)

Not metabolized by liver

FIGURE 4.6. Dosing and interaction information for paliperidone.

Olanzapine

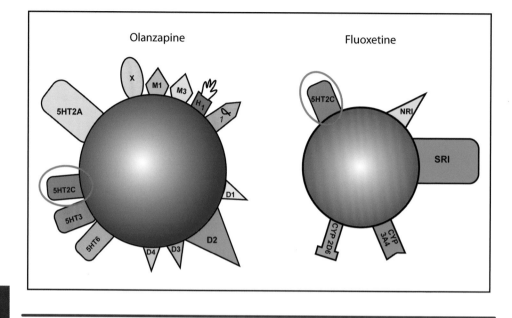

FIGURE 4.7. Olanzapine is a 5HT2A/D2 antagonist whose chemical structure is very similar to that of clozapine. Even at high doses, olanzapine only induces mild extrapyramidal side effects, emphasizing its atypical nature. Even though olanzapine has M1, H1, and alpha 1 antagonistic properties it is not as sedating as clozapine. It is one of the antipsychotics with the greatest cardiometabolic risk, as it leads to weight gain, increased fasting triglyceride levels, and increased insulin resistance. Olanzapine is often used at doses higher than what the packet insert suggests, as it often exhibits better efficacy and effectiveness at higher doses. Olanzapine appears to be effective at reducing affective and cognitive symptoms, a property most likely related in part to its 5HT2C antagonism. Olanzapine comes in different formulations, including oral disintegrating tablets and intramuscular formulations. Olanzapine was recently approved for the treatment of schizophrenia and manic or mixed episodes of bipolar I disorder in adolescents aged 13 to 17 years, and it has recently been approved as a four-week-long acting injectable.

Olanzapine: Tips and Pearls

Dosing

Formulation:
2.5, 5, 7.5, 10, 15, and 20 mg tablets; 5, 10, 15, and 20 mg orally disintegrating tablets; 10 mg vial of IM injection; 5 mg/mL IM formulation; olanzapine/fluoxetine (O/F) combo capsules (6 mg/25 mg; 6 mg/50 mg, 12 mg/25 mg, 12 mg/50 mg)

Dosage Range:
10–20 mg/day (oral or IM); O/F combo: 6–12 mg olanzapine/ 25–50 mg fluoxetine

Approved For:
Schizophrenia (maintenance of it and bipolar), acute agitation (IM), acute and mixed mania, bipolar depression, and treatment resistant depression (O/F combo), schizophrenia and manic or mixed episodes of bipolar I disorder in adolescents aged 13 to 17

Pearls

More may be more; doses above 15 mg/day useful for acutely ill/agitated patients; IM formulation can be given to initiate oral dosing; rapid onset without titration

Recently approved in adolescents aged 13 to 17

Pregnancy risk category C (some animal studies show adverse effects; no controlled studies in humans)

Side effects I

Weight Gain

unusual | not unusual | common | **problematic**

Sedation

unusual | not unusual | **common** | problematic

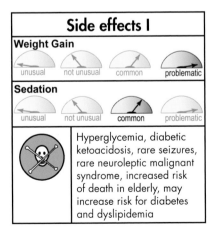

Hyperglycemia, diabetic ketoacidosis, rare seizures, rare neuroleptic malignant syndrome, increased risk of death in elderly, may increase risk for diabetes and dyslipidemia

Side effects II

CYP450 1A2 inhibitors increase and CYP450 1A2 inducers decrease its plasma levels; drug increases effects of antihypertensives and decreases DA agonist effects

Use with caution in patients with cardiac impairments

May need to lower dose in patients with renal impairments

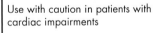

No dose adjustment needed for oral dose in patients with hepatic impairments; start lower for IM formulation

FIGURE 4.8. Dosing and interaction information for olanzapine.

Quetiapine

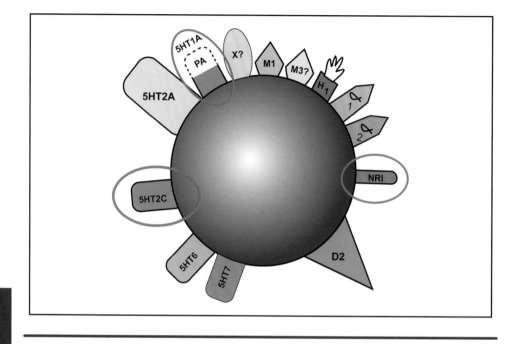

FIGURE 4.9. The 5HT2A/D2 antagonist quetiapine is chemically related to clozapine. Its active metabolite, norquetiapine, has unique features (red circles) that most likely add to quetiapine's efficacy. This very atypical antipsychotic exhibits rapid D2 dissociation, and therefore hardly any EPS and no prolactin elevation. The partial 5HT1A agonist feature of quetiapine and the norepinephrine reuptake-inhibiting and 5HT2C-blocking properties of norquetiapine are most likely responsible for its effectiveness at treating mood and cognitive disorders. Quetiapine is effective as a once-daily dose, and if given in the evening it will not induce daytime sedation. At moderate to high doses, both quetiapine and norquetiapine can induce weight gain due to histamine H1 blockade and 5HT2C blockade, respectively. Additionally, at these doses, quetiapine can increase triglyceride levels and insulin resistance, emphasizing the need to monitor patients if they are started on this atypical antipsychotic. Quetiapine is the only monotherapy approved for bipolar depression, and may also be useful for treatment-resistant depression. It has recently been approved as monotherapy for the treatment of schizophrenia in adolescents aged 13 to 17, and as monotherapy or an adjunct to lithium or divalproex for the acute treatment of manic episodes of bipolar disorder in children and adolescents aged 10 to 17.

Quetiapine: Tips and Pearls

Dosing

Formulation:
25, 50, 100, 200, 300, and 400 mg tablets
XR formulation: 200, 300, and 400 mg/ day once daily

Dosage Range:
150–750 mg/day (in 2 doses) for schizophrenia, 400–800 mg/day (in 2 doses) for acute bipolar mania 300–600 mg (in 1 dose at bedtime) for bipolar depression

Approved For:
Schizophrenia and maintenance of schizophrenia, acute mania, depressive episodes of bipolar disorder, schizophrenia and manic or mixed episodes of bipolar I disorder in adolescents aged 13 to 17, XR formulation approved as add-on treatment for depression, monotherapy or adjunct to lithium or divalproex for the acute treatment of manic episodes of bipolar disorder in children and adolescents aged 10 to 17

Side effects I

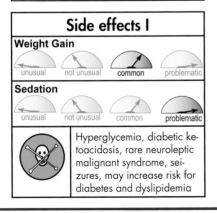

Pearls

More may be much more: is often underdosed, but even low doses can be sedating; no motor side effects; no prolactin elevation

Recently approved for children and adolescents (age 10 to 17 for acute manic episodes in bipolar disorder, age 13 to 17 for schizophrenia)

Pregnancy risk category C (some animal studies show adverse effects; no controlled studies in humans)

Side effects II

CYP450 3A4 and 2D6 inhibitors raise its levels, but dosage adjustment not necessary; drug increases effects of antihypertensives

Use with caution; orthostatic hypotension possible

Downward dose adjustment may be needed in patients with renal impairments

No dose adjustment needed in patients with hepatic impairments

FIGURE 4.10. Dosing and interaction information for quetiapine.

Ziprasidone

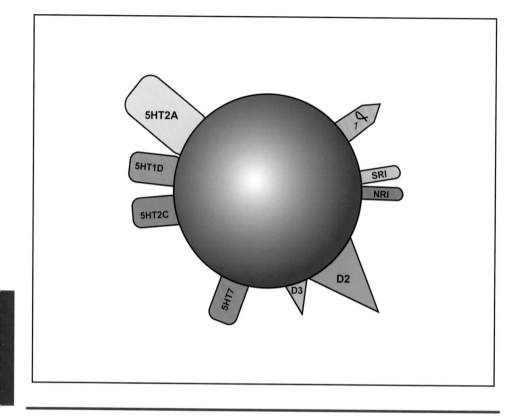

FIGURE 4.11. Compared to the atypical antipsychotics presented so far, ziprasidone is a chemically different compound with interesting pharmacology. Due to its 5HT2A/D2 blocking capability, it reduces the risk of EPS and elevated prolactin levels. Ziprasidone has been shown to treat both positive and negative symptoms. In cases of acute psychosis, the intramuscular formulation is highly effective. Rapid dose escalation to middle to high doses has been proven most effective. Ziprasidone's most differentiating feature is that is does not induce weight gain, dyslipidemia, elevation of fasting triglycerides, or insulin resistance.

The 5HT1D antagonist actions combined with the 5HT and NE reuptake blocking properties might contribute to the absence of weight gain induction by ziprasidone, as well as its potential antidepressant and anxiolytic properties.

Ziprasidone: Tips and Pearls

Dosing

Formulation:
20, 40, 60, and 80 mg capsules; 20 mg/mL injection

Dosage Range:
40–200 mg/day orally in divided doses (must be given with food), 10–20 mg intramuscularly

Approved For:
Schizophrenia, delaying relapse in schizophrenia, acute agitation in schizophrenia (IM), acute mania/mixed mania, maintenance treatment of bipolar disorder, mania in adolescents (ages 10–17)

Pearls

It is often underdosed; activation occurs at 20–40 mg 2X/day and is reduced at 60–80 mg 2X/day; food doubles bioavailability; it may improve symptoms of depression as well as mania in patients with dysphoric mania

Recently approved for children and adolescents (age 10 to 17 mania)

Pregnancy risk category C (some animal studies show adverse effects; no controlled studies in humans)

Side effects I

Weight Gain

| unusual | not unusual | common | problematic |

Sedation

| unusual | not unusual | common | problematic |

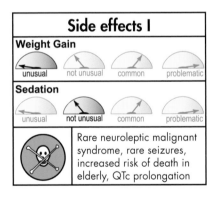

Rare neuroleptic malignant syndrome, rare seizures, increased risk of death in elderly, QTc prolongation

Side effects II

Not affected by CYP450 enzymes; drug increases effects of antihypertensives and decreases DA agonist effects; may enhance QTc prolongation of other drugs that enhance QTc prolongation

Contraindicated in patients with QTc prolongation

No dose adjustment necessary in patients with renal impairments

No dose adjustment necessary in patients with hepatic impairments

---

FIGURE 4.12. Dosing and interaction information for ziprasidone.

Aripiprazole

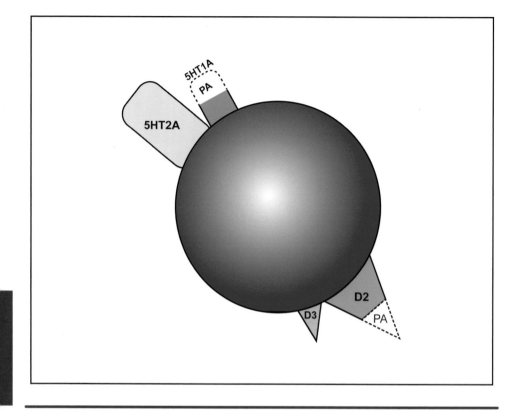

FIGURE 4.13. Aripiprazole is the first atypical antipsychotic with D2 partial agonist properties. Its 5HT2A and 5HT1A features may be the reason for its increased tolerability and efficacy. Aripiprazole is effective at treating positive and manic symptoms. Its benefits also lie in its many different formulations (tablets, disintegrating tablets, liquid, and IM formulations). Aripiprazole is usually devoid of sedative side effects, and can even be activating. For some patients aripiprazole is either too close to a full antagonist, or too close to a full agonist. In both cases, dose adjustment and the timing of administration can ameliorate these symptoms.

Similarly to ziprasidone, aripiprazole causes little to no weight gain, most likely because it lacks 5HT2C and histamine H1 properties. Additionally, aripiprazole does not seem to induce dyslipidemia, increase fasting triglyceride levels, or increase insulin resistance. Thus aripiprazole has a lower cardiometabolic risk.

Aripiprazole: Tips and Pearls

 ## Dosing

Formulation:
2, 5, 10, 15, 20, 30 mg tablets; 1mg/
mL oral solution; 10 and 15 mg orally
disintegrating tablets; 9.75 mg/1.3 mL
single-dose vial injection

Dosage Range:
15–30 mg/day; solution doses can be
substituted for tablet doses on a mg-per-
mg basis up to 25 mg

Approved For:
Schizophrenia (adults and adolescents),
maintaining stability in schizophrenia,
acute mania/mixed mania, bipolar
maintenance; adjunctive treatment to
antidepressants for Major Depressive
Disorder in adults, irritability in autistic
children (age 6 to 17)

Side effects I

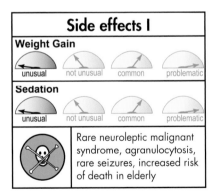

| | Rare neuroleptic malignant syndrome, agranulocytosis, rare seizures, increased risk of death in elderly |

Pearls

 May be activating; no diabetes
or dyslipidemia risk; favorable
tolerability profile; for some, less
may be more, for others more may
be more; may be useful in bipolar
depression

 Approved for schizophrenia (age
13 to 17), bipolar (age 10 to 17),
and irritability in autistic children
(age 6 to 17)

Pregnancy risk category C (some
animal studies show adverse
effects; no controlled studies in
humans)

Side effects II

 CYP450 3A4 or 2D6 inhibitors
increase its plasma levels, and
CYP450 3A4 inducers lower
them; drug increases effects of
antihypertensives and decreases
DA agonist effects

Use with caution due to risk of
orthostatic hypotension

No dose adjustment needed in
patients with renal impairments

No dose adjustment needed in
patients with hepatic impairments

FIGURE 4.14. Dosing and interaction information for aripiprazole.

Zotepine

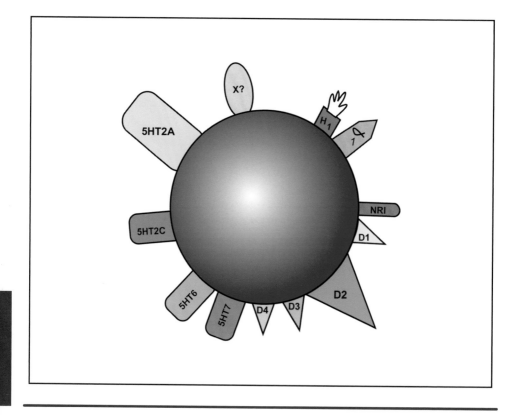

FIGURE 4.15. This 5HT2A/D2 antagonist has a chemical structure similar to that of clozapine, but different pharmacology. Despite its 5HT2A antagonism it can lead to EPS and elevation of prolactin levels. It might also induce weight gain and sedation, and it probably increases the risk for insulin resistance, dyslipidemia, and diabetes.

Another side effect of zotepine is its tendency to increase QTc prolongation. Due to its norepinephrine reuptake inhibition, zotepine has the potential for antidepressant actions.

Zotepine: Tips and Pearls

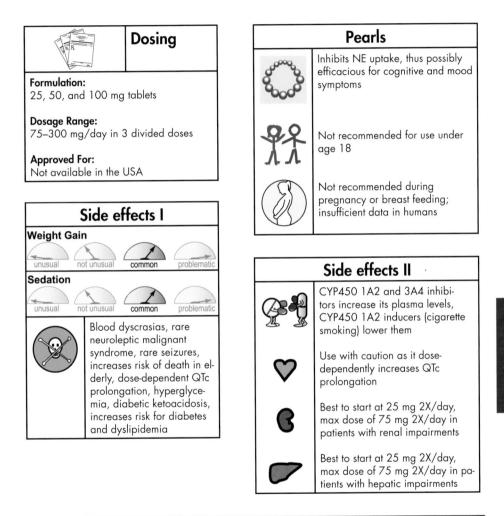

Dosing

Formulation:
25, 50, and 100 mg tablets

Dosage Range:
75–300 mg/day in 3 divided doses

Approved For:
Not available in the USA

Side effects I

Weight Gain

unusual | not unusual | common | problematic

Sedation

unusual | not unusual | common | problematic

Blood dyscrasias, rare neuroleptic malignant syndrome, rare seizures, increases risk of death in elderly, dose-dependent QTc prolongation, hyperglycemia, diabetic ketoacidosis, increases risk for diabetes and dyslipidemia

Pearls

Inhibits NE uptake, thus possibly efficacious for cognitive and mood symptoms

Not recommended for use under age 18

Not recommended during pregnancy or breast feeding; insufficient data in humans

Side effects II

CYP450 1A2 and 3A4 inhibitors increase its plasma levels, CYP450 1A2 inducers (cigarette smoking) lower them

Use with caution as it dose-dependently increases QTc prolongation

Best to start at 25 mg 2X/day, max dose of 75 mg 2X/day in patients with renal impairments

Best to start at 25 mg 2X/day, max dose of 75 mg 2X/day in patients with hepatic impairments

FIGURE 4.16. Dosing and interaction information for zotepine.

Perospirone

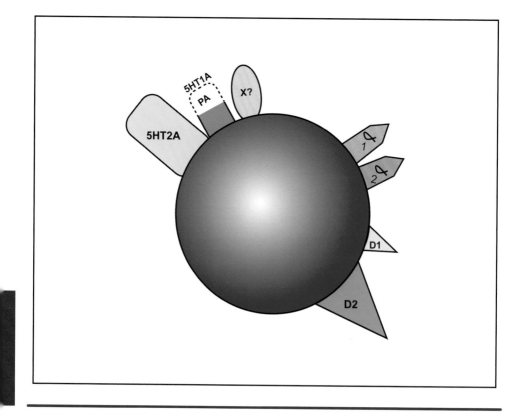

FIGURE 4.17. Perospirone is a 5HT2A/D2 antagonist with 5HT1A partial agonist properties, which most likely contribute to its efficacy. It is approved and marketed in Japan.

Perospirone: Tips and Pearls

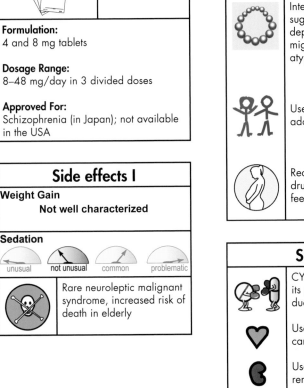

Dosing

Formulation:
4 and 8 mg tablets

Dosage Range:
8–48 mg/day in 3 divided doses

Approved For:
Schizophrenia (in Japan); not available in the USA

Side effects I

Weight Gain
   Not well characterized

Sedation

unusual   not unusual   common   problematic

Rare neuroleptic malignant syndrome, increased risk of death in elderly

Pearls

Interactions at 5HT1A receptors suggest possible efficacy for depression and anxiety symptoms, might have worse EPS than other atypical antipsychotics

Use with caution in children and adolescents

Recommended to discontinue drug during pregnancy or breast feeding

Side effects II

CYP450 3A4 inhibitors increase its plasma levels; CYP450 3A4 inducers decrease its plasma levels

Use with caution in patients with cardiac impairments

Use with caution in patients with renal impairments

Use with caution in patients with hepatic impairments

FIGURE 4.18. Dosing and interaction information for perospirone.

Sertindole

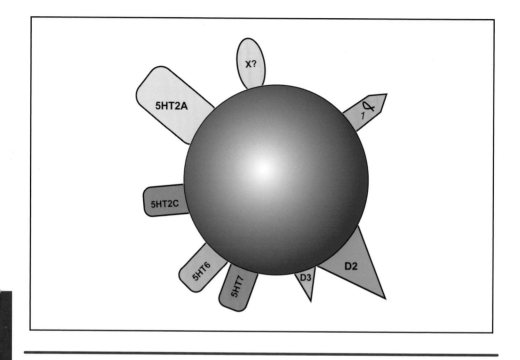

FIGURE 4.19. Sertindole is one of the newer atypical antipsychotics with 5HT2A/D2 antagonist properties. Because some patients, who do not benefit from other antipsychotics, may benefit from sertindole despite having the potential for QTc prolongation, sertindole is being carefully introduced into clinical practice in some countries along with careful dosing and EKG monitoring guidelines. Specifically, patients should have a pretreatment EKG as well as serum potassium and magnesium levels determined. Sertindole should not be started in the presence of hypokalemia or hypomagnesemia, or at QTc>450 in men, or >470 in women. EKGs should be repeated when reaching steady state, at 3 weeks after treatment initiation, then every 3 months during treatment, prior to and after any dose increase, after addition of any drug that can affect the concentration of sertindole, and upon reaching a dose of 16 mg. Sertindole should be discontinued if QTc>500 msec and should be reevaluated if palpitations, convulsions, or a syncope become apparent. This medication is aimed at patients who are intolerant to at least one other antipsychotic, when the potential benefits outweigh the risks.

Sertindole: Tips and Pearls

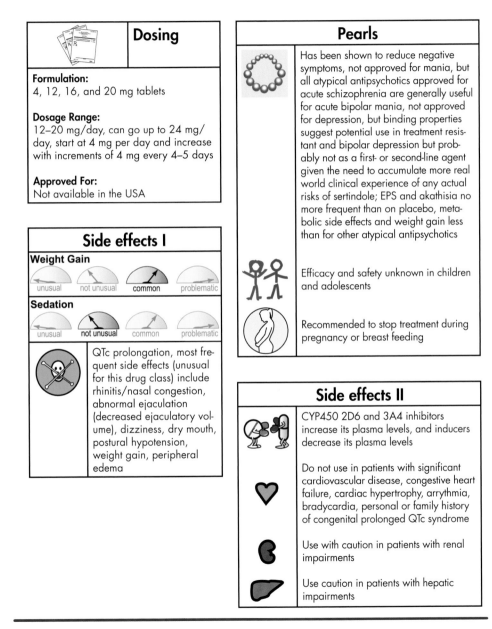

Dosing

Formulation:
4, 12, 16, and 20 mg tablets

Dosage Range:
12–20 mg/day, can go up to 24 mg/day, start at 4 mg per day and increase with increments of 4 mg every 4–5 days

Approved For:
Not available in the USA

Side effects I

Weight Gain

unusual / not unusual / **common** / problematic

Sedation

unusual / **not unusual** / common / problematic

QTc prolongation, most frequent side effects (unusual for this drug class) include rhinitis/nasal congestion, abnormal ejaculation (decreased ejaculatory volume), dizziness, dry mouth, postural hypotension, weight gain, peripheral edema

Pearls

Has been shown to reduce negative symptoms, not approved for mania, but all atypical antipsychotics approved for acute schizophrenia are generally useful for acute bipolar mania, not approved for depression, but binding properties suggest potential use in treatment resistant and bipolar depression but probably not as a first- or second-line agent given the need to accumulate more real world clinical experience of any actual risks of sertindole; EPS and akathisia no more frequent than on placebo, metabolic side effects and weight gain less than for other atypical antipsychotics

Efficacy and safety unknown in children and adolescents

Recommended to stop treatment during pregnancy or breast feeding

Side effects II

CYP450 2D6 and 3A4 inhibitors increase its plasma levels, and inducers decrease its plasma levels

Do not use in patients with significant cardiovascular disease, congestive heart failure, cardiac hypertrophy, arrythmia, bradycardia, personal or family history of congenital prolonged QTc syndrome

Use with caution in patients with renal impairments

Use caution in patients with hepatic impairments

FIGURE 4.20. Dosing and interaction information for sertindole.

Loxapine:
Conventional or Low-Dose Atypical?

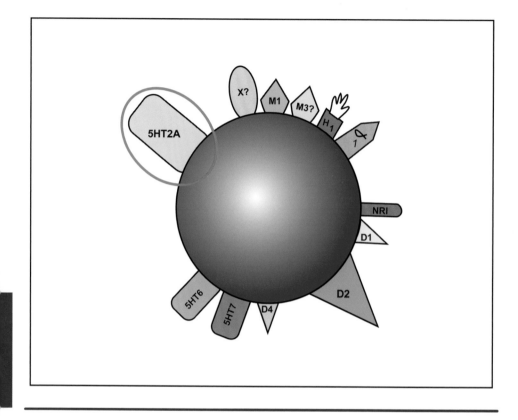

FIGURE 4.21. Although loxapine has a chemical structure similar to that of clozapine and exhibits 5HT2A/D2 antagonism, it is often classified as a conventional antipsychotic, as it can lead to EPS and prolactin elevation. Apparently, however, low doses of loxapine can be more "atypical."

Although loxapine usually does not lead to weight gain, it might present a cardiometabolic risk. Loxapine has an intramuscular formulation, and its metabolite amoxapine is a tricyclic antidepressant.

Loxapine: Tips and Pearls

 Dosing

Formulation:
6.8 mg, 13.6 mg, 34 mg, and
68.1 mg loxapine succinate capsules
(equivalent of 5, 10, 25, 50 mg loxapine, respectively); 25 mg/mL oral liquid;
50 mg/mL injection

Dosage Range:
60–100 mg/day in divided doses

Approved For:
Schizophrenia

Pearls

 May be an atypical antipsychotic at lower doses; one active
metabolite is an antidepressant
(amoxapine)

 Safety and efficacy not established in children and adolescents,
2nd-line treatment after atypical
antipsychotic

 Not recommended during
pregnancy or breast feeding;
insufficient data in humans

Side effects I

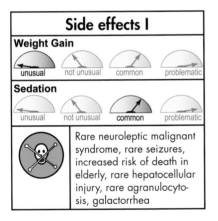

Weight Gain

unusual   not unusual   common   problematic

Sedation

unusual   not unusual   **common**   problematic

Rare neuroleptic malignant
syndrome, rare seizures,
increased risk of death in
elderly, rare hepatocellular
injury, rare agranulocytosis, galactorrhea

Side effects II

In combo with lorazepam induces
respiratory depression; decreases
effects of DA agonists; decreases
BP in combo with epinephrine

Use with caution in patients with
cardiac impairments

Use with caution in patients with
renal impairments

Use with caution in patients with
hepatic impairments

FIGURE 4.22. Dosing and interaction information for loxapine.

Cyamemazine:
Conventional or Low-Dose Atypical?

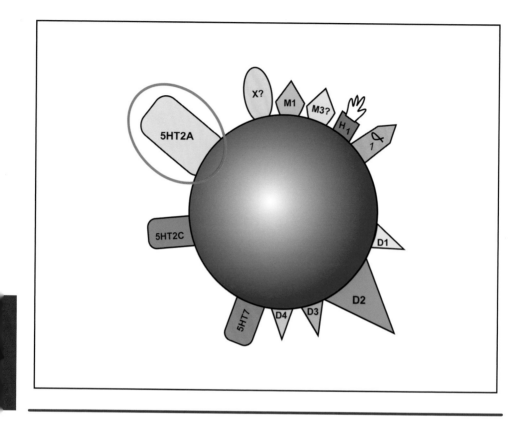

FIGURE 4.23. Originally developed as a conventional antipsychotic, especially at high doses, cyamemazine was later discovered to have 5HT2A antagonistic properties, especially at lower doses.

This compound has high popularity in Europe, especially France, where it is used to treat anxiety associated with psychosis. Little information is available on its cardio-metabolic and weight gain risks.

Cyamemazine: Tips and Pearls

Dosing

Formulation:
25, 100 mg tablets; 40 mg/mL oral solution; 50 mg/5 mL injection

Dosage Range:
50–300 mg at bedtime (psychosis);
1–4 mg/kg/day (children 6 and older);
25–100 mg/day for injections

Approved For:
Not available in the USA

Pearls

 Low dose has anxiolytic action and rarely causes motor side effects or prolactin elevation

Used for severe behavioral disturbances in children and adolescents; oral solution preferred

Not recommended during pregnancy or breast feeding

Side effects I

Weight Gain

unusual   not unusual   common   problematic

Sedation

unusual   not unusual   **common**   problematic

Rare neuroleptic malignant syndrome, rare seizures, rare agranulocytosis, jaundice, QTc prolongation

Side effects II

Decreases effects of DA agonists; decreases BP in combo with epinephrine; increases effects of antihypertensive drugs

Cardiovascular toxicity and orthostatic hypotension

Use with caution in patients with renal impairments

Use with caution in patients with hepatic impairments

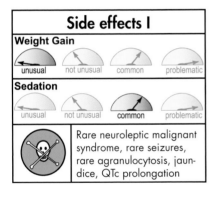

FIGURE 4.24. Dosing and interaction information for cyamemazine.

Amisulpride

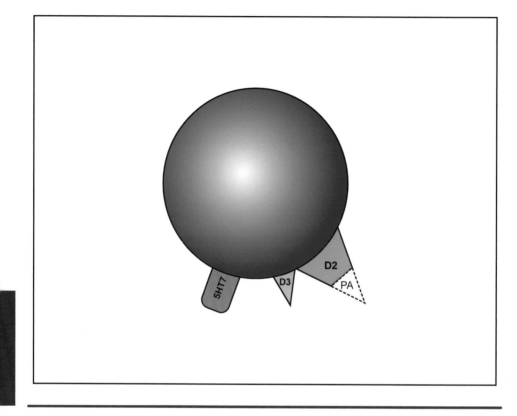

FIGURE 4.25. Amisulpride was developed in Europe before the concept of D2 partial agonism was fully accepted. It does not have any affinity at the 5HT2A receptor, and its side effect profile has not been fully investigated. It has recently been shown to have potent 5HT7 antagonist properties.

It might lead to QTc prolongation and has been shown to induce prolactin elevation.

Amisulpride: Tips and Pearls

Dosing

Formulation:
50, 100, 200, and 400 mg tablets;
100 mg/mL oral solution; IM formulation

Dosage Range:
400–800 mg/day in 2 doses (schizophrenia); 50–300 mg/day (mainly negative symptoms)

Approved For:
Acute and chronic schizophrenia (in Europe), not available in the USA

Pearls

Efficacy in patients with negative symptoms as low doses are activating; some evidence for usefulness in depression; clinical actions may be linked to 5HT7 antagonist actions and or D2/D3 partial agonist actions; increases prolactin; could result in amenorrhea

Efficacy and safety not established under age 18

Not recommended during pregnancy or breast feeding

Side effects I

Weight Gain

unusual | **not unusual** | common | problematic

Sedation

unusual | not unusual | **common** | problematic

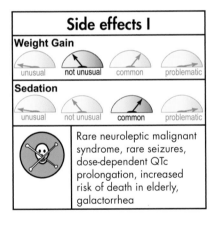

Rare neuroleptic malignant syndrome, rare seizures, dose-dependent QTc prolongation, increased risk of death in elderly, galactorrhea

Side effects II

Increases effects of antihypertensive drugs and decreases effects of DA agonists; as it is weakly metabolized, few drug interactions exist

Dose-dependent prolongation of QTc interval

Use with caution if renal insufficiency is present; drug can accumulate, as it is eliminated through the kidneys

Use with caution in patients with hepatic impairments

FIGURE 4.26. Dosing and interaction information for amisulpride.

Sulpiride:
Conventional or Low-Dose Atypical?

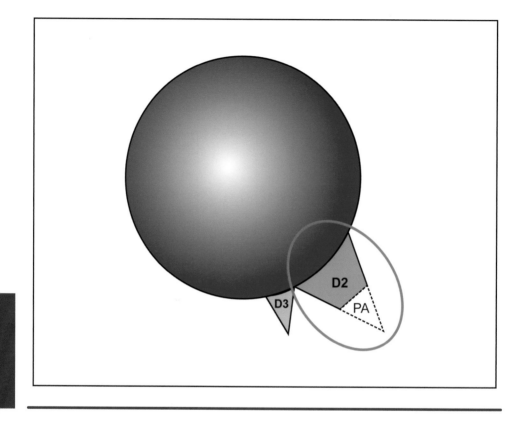

FIGURE 4.27. Sulpiride is structurally related to amisulpride. It too will lead to EPS and prolactin elevation at high doses, but it exhibits antidepressant actions and efficacy for negative symptoms at low doses.

Sulpiride: Tips and Pearls

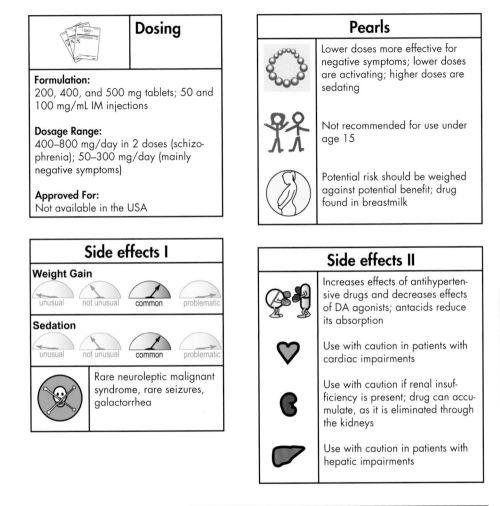

Dosing

Formulation:
200, 400, and 500 mg tablets; 50 and 100 mg/mL IM injections

Dosage Range:
400–800 mg/day in 2 doses (schizophrenia); 50–300 mg/day (mainly negative symptoms)

Approved For:
Not available in the USA

Pearls

Lower doses more effective for negative symptoms; lower doses are activating; higher doses are sedating

Not recommended for use under age 15

Potential risk should be weighed against potential benefit; drug found in breastmilk

Side effects I

Weight Gain

unusual · not unusual · **common** · problematic

Sedation

unusual · not unusual · **common** · problematic

Rare neuroleptic malignant syndrome, rare seizures, galactorrhea

Side effects II

Increases effects of antihypertensive drugs and decreases effects of DA agonists; antacids reduce its absorption

Use with caution in patients with cardiac impairments

Use with caution if renal insufficiency is present; drug can accumulate, as it is eliminated through the kidneys

Use with caution in patients with hepatic impairments

FIGURE 4.28. Dosing and interaction information for sulpiride.

Iloperidone

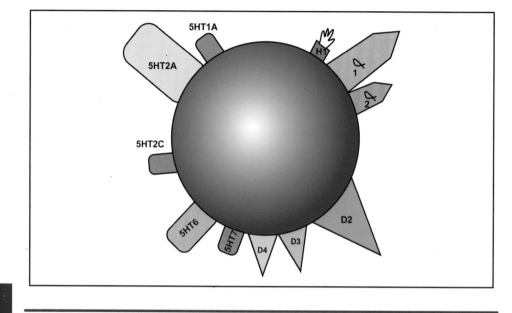

FIGURE 4.29. Iloperidone is one of the newer atypical antipsychotics with 5HT2A/D2 antagonistic properties. There is only limited registration data and real world clinical experience, but slow titration according to product label seems prudent until additional information is available. In patients developing orthostasis, or when adding to or switching from another drug with alpha 1 antagonist properties, it may be necessary to titrate even slower. Patients most sensitive to orthostasis include the young, the elderly, those with cardiovascular problems, and those with concomitant vasoactive drugs. However, realistically this slow dosing could lead to delayed onset of antipsychotic effects, so once more is known about iloperidone dosing may proceed more rapidly and possibly switch to once daily, once greater confidence about this drug develops. The 18 to 33 hour half-life also theoretically supports once daily dosing as a possibility. The dose may need to be reduced by half in the presence of potent 2D6 inhibitors such as paroxetine, fluoxetine, and duloxetine. A four-week depot preparation is in clinical testing. The doses used in clinical trials have been up to 32 mg/day, with an anticipated dose range of 12–24 mg/day given in divided doses. Similar side effects have been observed throughout the dosage range. Iloperidone exhibits dose-dependent QTc prolongation.

Iloperidone: Tips and Pearls

 Dosing

Formulation:
1, 2, 4, 6, 8, 10, and 12 mg tablets, may be available in starter/titration packs in some countries

Dosage Range:
12–24 mg/day for actue schizophrenia in adults; medication needs to be titrated; doses up to 32 mg have been studied, but not approved

Approved For:
Acute treatment of schizophrenia in adults

Side effects I

Weight Gain

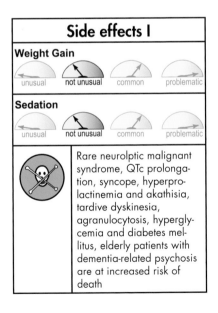

unusual | not unusual | common | problematic

Sedation

unusual | not unusual | common | problematic

Rare neurolptic malignant syndrome, QTc prolongation, syncope, hyperprolactinemia and akathisia, tardive dyskinesia, agranulocytosis, hyperglycemia and diabetes mellitus, elderly patients with dementia-related psychosis are at increased risk of death

Pearls

Can lead to weight loss in some patients; titrate slowly to avoid orthostatic hypertension; low extrapyramidal side effects, including little or no akathisia but real world clinical experience needs to confirm this; not approved for mania but all atypical antipsychotics approved for acute treatment of schizophrenia have proven effective in acute treatment of mania as well; metabolic and weight gain profile seems comparable to risperidone, and greater than ziprasidone; potent alpha 1 blocking properties suggest potential utility in PTSD (e.g., nightmares, as for prazosin); binding properties suggest theoretical efficacy in depression

Efficacy and safety not established in children and adolescents

 Pregnancy risk category C (some animal studies show adverse effects; no controlled studies in humans); recommended to stop breast feeding

Side effects II

CYP450 2D6 and 3A4 inhibitors increase its plasma levels

Contraindicated to take with another drug that causes QTc prolongation

No dose adjustment needed in patients with renal impairments, as drug is highly metabolized

Not recommended for patients with hepatic impairments

FIGURE 4.30. Dosing and interaction information for sulpiride.

Asenapine

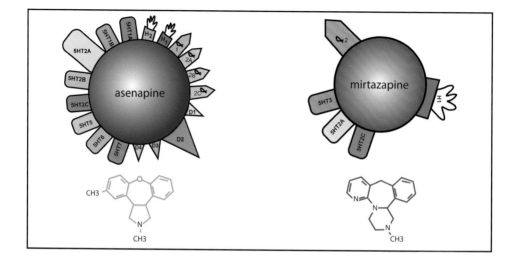

FIGURE 4.31. Asenapine is one of the newer atypical antipsychotics with 5HT2A/D2 antagonist properties. It has a chemical structure related to the antidepressant mirtazapine, and shares all the pharmacological binding properties of mirtazapine, plus others. Antagonist actions at 5HT2C receptors and at alpha 2 receptors suggest potential antidepressant properties, but additional research is needed to determine this. There is only limited registration data and real world clinical experience, but according to product label, no dose titration seems necessary. Thus the initial and maintenance dose for bipolar mania is 10 mg twice daily, and can be reduced to 5 mg twice daily. The initial and maintenance dose for acute schizophrenia is only 5 mg twice daily. In practice, some patients with acute schizophrenia may be titrated up to 10 mg twice daily, but with limited real world clinical experience the dose response for asenapine remains an open issue. Once daily use is theoretically possible due to the 13–39 hour half-life, however this may be limited because of the sublingual formulation. As asenapine is not absorbed after swallowing (<2% bioavailable orally), it must be administered sublingually, which increases the bioavailability to 35%. A common side effect is hypoesthesia, and patients may not eat or drink for 10 minutes following sublingual administration to avoid the drug being washed into the stomach where it will not be absorbed. Sublingual administration may require prescribing asenapine to reliable and compliant patients, or those who have someone who can supervise drug administration.

Asenapine: Tips and Pearls

Dosing

Formulation:
5 and 10 mg sublingual tablets

Dosage Range:
For schizophrenia: 5 mg sublingually twice daily; for bipolar disorder: 10 mg sublingually twice a day

Approved For:
Acute treatment of schizophrenia in adults, acute treatment of manic and mixed episodes associated with bipolar I disorder in adults

Pearls

 Tablets dissolve in saliva under tongue within seconds, and should not be swallowed; drinking and eating should be avoided for 10 minutes after administration; not approved for depression but binding properties suggest potential use in treatment resistant and bipolar depression; an early study suggested better efficacy for negative symptoms, but this has not been replicated

Efficacy and safety not established in children and adolescents

Pregnancy risk category C (some animal studies show adverse effects; no controlled studies in humans); recommended to stop breast feeding

Side effects I

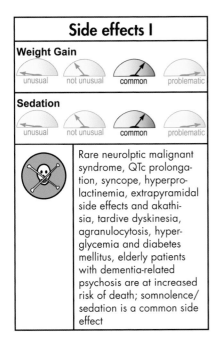

Weight Gain

unusual | not unusual | **common** | problematic

Sedation

unusual | not unusual | **common** | problematic

Rare neurolptic malignant syndrome, QTc prolongation, syncope, hyperprolactinemia, extrapyramidal side effects and akathisia, tardive dyskinesia, agranulocytosis, hyperglycemia and diabetes mellitus, elderly patients with dementia-related psychosis are at increased risk of death; somnolence/sedation is a common side effect

Side effects II

CYP450 1A2 inhibitors increase its plasma levels; asenapine is a weak inhibitor of CYP450 2D6, and causes an increase in paroxetine levels (a CYP450 substrate and inhibitor) when coadministered; asenapine is a substrate for 1A2

Use with caution in patients with cardiac impairments

No dose adjustment necessary in patients with renal impairment

Not recommended in patients with severe hepatic impairment

FIGURE 4.32. Dosing and interaction information for asenapine.

Lurasidone

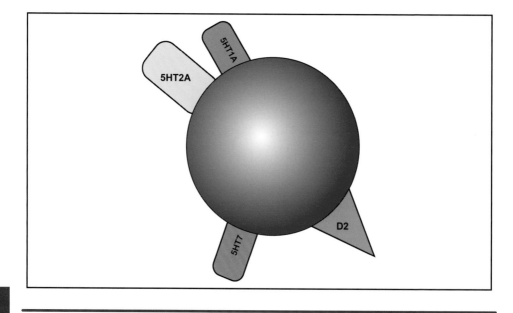

FIGURE 4.33. Lurasidone is one of the newer atypical antipsychotics with 5HT2A/ D2 and potent 5HT7 antagonist properties and is in late stage clinical testing for schizophrenia and bipolar mania. This compound exhibits high affinity for both 5HT7 and 5HT1A receptors and these serotonergic properties may explain some of lurasidone's clinical actions. It also has minimal affinity for alpha 1 and alpha 2A adrenergic receptors, dopamine D1 and D3 receptors, and serotonin 5HT2C receptors. Interestingly, lurasidone lacks affinity for H1 histamine receptors, and for the M1 cholinergic receptors, which enables starting treatment at the therapeutically effective dose, allowing for a rapid onset of efficacy. Preliminary studies have shown that a dose of 80 mg/day is an effective treatment for acute exacerbation of schizophrenia. Doses of 40–120 mg/day have proven effective in clinical trials, and lurasidone appears to have a benign metabolic profile without affecting QTc prolongation. According to early results of clinical trials, once a day administration is possible and results in low extrapyramidal side effects, akathisia, metabolic, or weight gain side effects. Lurasidone is currently in phase III clinical trials for the treatment of acute and chronic schizophrenia, as well as monotherapy and adjunctive treatment of bipolar depression. Actions at 5HT7 and 5HT1A receptors suggest potential antidepressant and pro-cognitive actions, but this requires confirmation in clinical trials and real world clinical experience.

Cariprazine

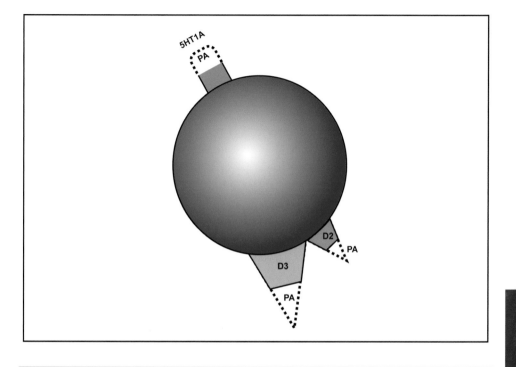

FIGURE 4.34. Cariprazine is a dopamine partial agonist in clinical testing, the only agent with D3 preferring over D2 affinity, with both actions being partial agonist actions rather than antagonist actions. This compound is in testing for schizophrenia, acute bipolar mania, bipolar depression, and treatment-resistant depression, and has provided some preliminary evidence of clinical efficacy in acute schizophrenia and mania. Cariprazine seems to be more of an agonist than the related partial agonist aripiprazole, but less of an agonist within the agonist spectrum than bifeprunox, a related agent that did not receive FDA approval (as it demonstrated less efficacy than comparator antipsychotics, was too activating, had a slow dose titration, and caused nausea and vomiting). In theory, carpiprazine may be preferred at higher doses for mania and schizophrenia to emphasize its antagonist actions and at lower doses for depression to emphasize its agonist actions. Dosing, efficacy, and side effects are still under investigation, but little weight gain or metabolic problems have been identified thus far. This compound has two long to very long lasting active metabolites with potential for development as a weekly or biweekly or even monthly oral depot.

The Future of Antipsychotics

Table 4.1	
Compounds	**Properties and Notes**
Glycine agonists	Glycine, d-serine, or its analogue d-cycloserine bind to the glycine site of the NMDA receptor, and could potentially stimulate the NMDA receptors enough to overcompensate for their hypothetical hypofunction; d-cycloserine is effective at treating negative and cognitive symptoms
GlyT1 inhibitors	Glycine transporter (GlyT1) inhibitors such as sarcosine block reuptake of glycine, thus increasing its synaptic availability. This could then lead to enhancement of NMDA neurotransmission and reversal of the hypofunctioning of NMDA receptors
mGluR agents	mGluR2/3 presynaptic receptor agonists could potentially decrease glutamate release; mGluR1 postsynaptic receptor agents can hypothetically modulate glutamate receptors and enhance postsynaptic NMDA-mediated neurotransmission
AMPA-kines	Positive allosteric modulators (PAMs) of this other glutamate receptor subtype, the AMPA receptor, can potentially enhance cognitive functioning
Sigma 1 agonists / antagonists	Sigma 1 receptors are linked to the psychotomimetic actions of PCP and regulate NMDA receptors; it is not yet known whether an agonist or antagonist would be best in schizophrenia; this is the "sigma enigma"
New 5HT agents	5HT2A-selective antagonists/inverse agonists, 5HT1A agonists/antagonists, and 5HT2C agonists/antagonists are being investigated to improve cognitive effects and reduce side effects; 5HT6 antagonists might be beneficial by increasing brain-derived neurotrophic factor; 5HT7 antagonists could be beneficial for sleep and anxiety
New DA agents	D3 antagonists or partial agonists could potentially be useful to treat negative and cognitive symptoms and to alleviate stimulant abuse; D1 agonists and DA transporter inhibitors may be useful pro-cognitive agents
Acetylcholine-linked agents	Partial agonists at alpha-7-nicotinic cholinergic receptors may be pro-cognitive agents; varenicline, an alpha-4 beta-2 partial agonist, is approved for smoking cessation and could be beneficial in schizophrenia
Peptide-linked agents	Neurokinin antagonists have been tested, with unclear benefits; antagonists of neurotensin, which is colocalized with DA, are thought to reduce positive symptoms without inducing EPS; cholecystokinin is also colocalized with DA, but no clear data on any compound are available

Chapter 5

Schizophrenia Pharmacy and Switching Strategies

Figuring out how to treat schizophrenia in different patients can be challenging. Different "pharmacies" are presented in this chapter that can be useful in the search for an effective treatment plan. Practical switching strategies are also presented that will aid in properly changing medications in patients when different treatments are required.

Abbreviations Used in this Chapter	
AChEI	acetylcholinesterase inhibitor
BZ	benzodiazepine
D2	dopamine 2 antagonist
DPA	dopamine 2 partial antagonist
SDA	serotonin 2A and dopamine 2 antagonist
NRI	norepinephrine reuptake inhibitor
SSRI	selective serotonin reuptake inhibitor

The Puzzle of Schizophrenia

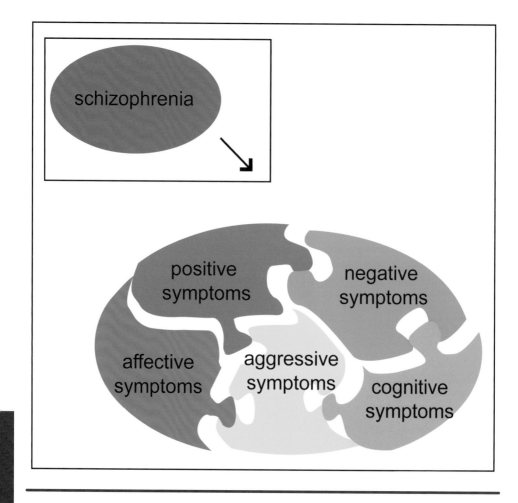

FIGURE 5.1. Schizophrenia is an aggregation of different symptoms, including positive, negative, aggressive, affective, and cognitive ones. One medication may not treat all of a patient's symptoms effectively.

Likewise, a patient might not present with the full panoply of symptoms and might thus require specific treatment. Thus it is beneficial to know which medications are more efficacious at treating different symptom dimensions.

Treating Positive Symptoms

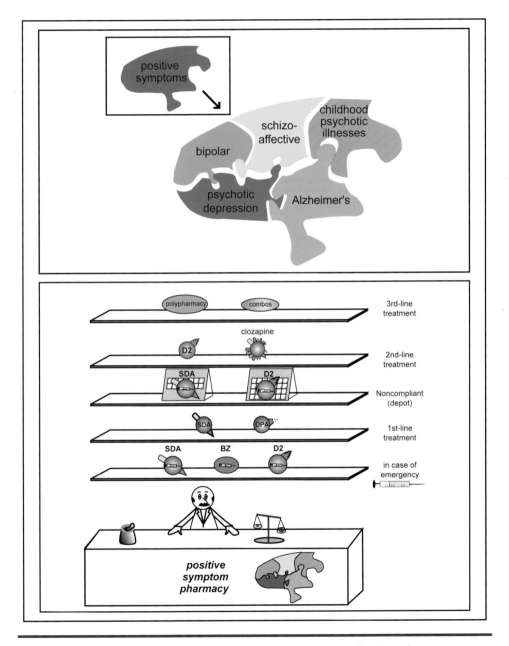

FIGURE 5.2. The best treatments for the positive symptoms of schizophrenia.

Treating Negative Symptoms

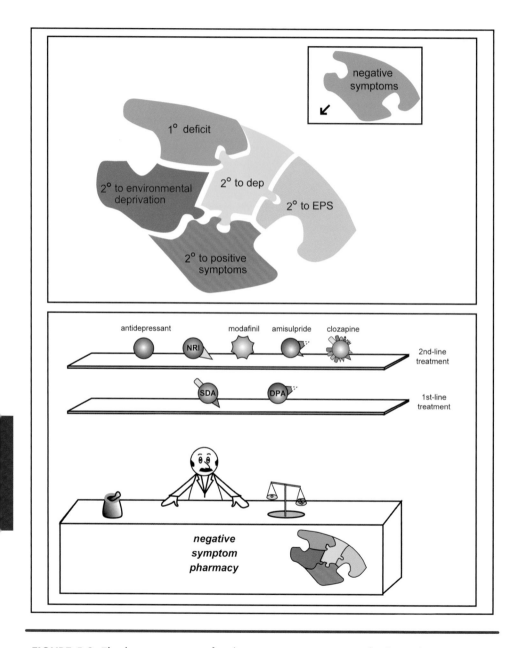

FIGURE 5.3. The best treatments for the negative symptoms of schizophrenia.

Treating Cognitive Symptoms

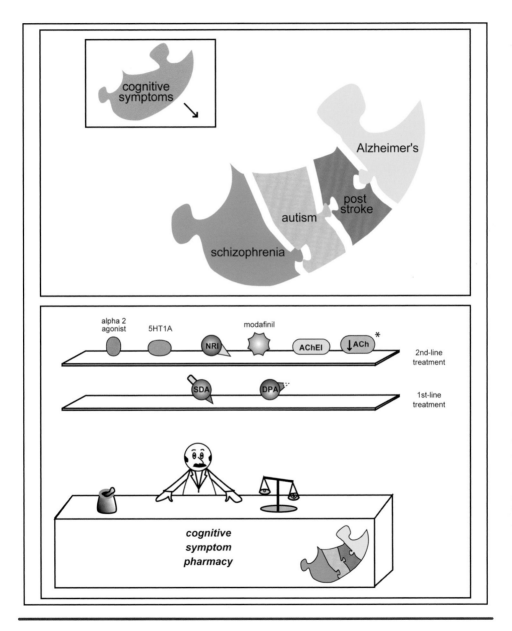

FIGURE 5.4. The best treatments for the cognitive symptoms of schizophrenia.
*↓ACh = decrease anticholinergics

Treating Aggressive Symptoms

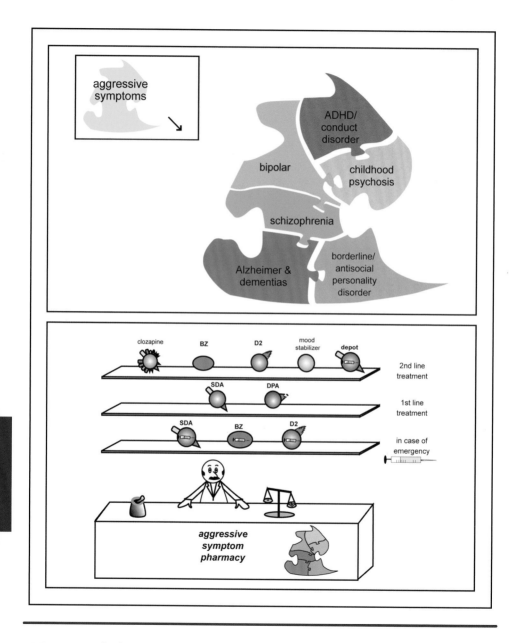

FIGURE 5.5. The best treatments for the aggressive symptoms of schizophrenia.

Treating Affective Symptoms

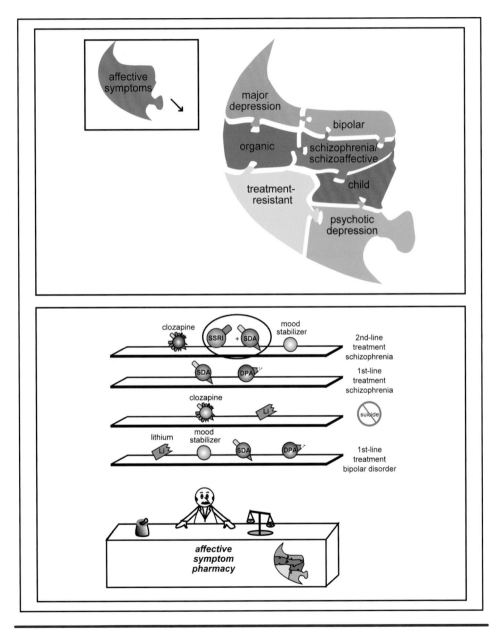

FIGURE 5.6. The best treatments for the affective symptoms of schizophrenia.

Treating Metabolic Issues

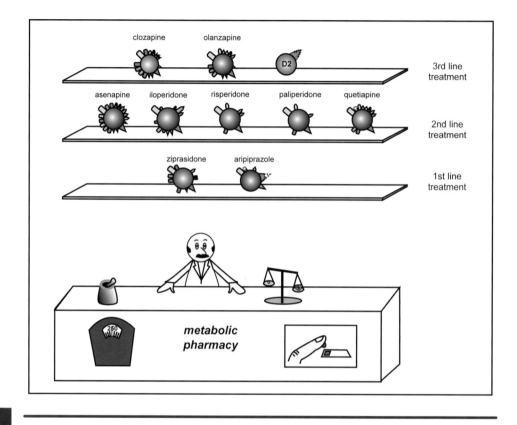

FIGURE 5.7. Aripiprazole and ziprasidone appear to have lower risks for cardio-metabolic problems and weight gain, and therefore represent the first-line treatment in the metabolic pharmacy. Risperidone, paliperidone, quetiapine, iloperidone, and asenapine are second-line treatment options as they carry an intermediate risk to gain weight and develop cardiometabolic side effects.

Olanzapine and clozapine have the highest risk of weight gain and therefore cardiometabolic disease, and should only be used as third-line treatment. Some of the conventional antipsychotics might actually carry less risk of cardiometabolic side effects, but more research is required.

Treating Sedation

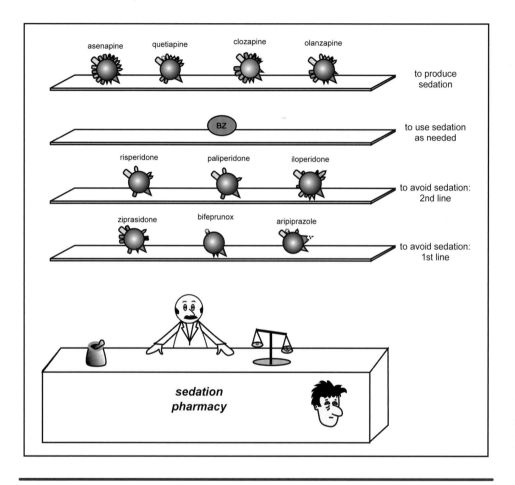

FIGURE 5.8. Ziprasidone and aripiprazole are the antipsychotics with the least tendency to induce sedation. Risperidone, paliperidone, and iloperidone have been known to induce sedation in some patients, but not in others.

If sedation is wanted, then compounds such as quetiapine, clozapine, olanzapine, or asenapine should be used. Augmentation with a benzodiazepine can also lead to sedation.

How Not to Switch Antipsychotics

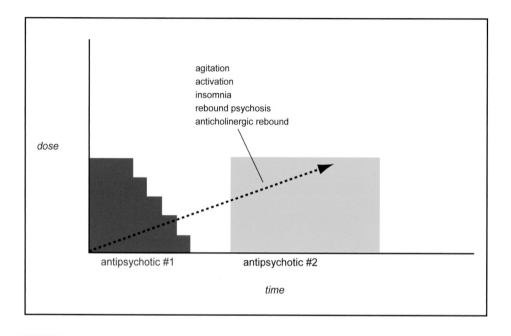

FIGURE 5.9. There are strategies for switching antipsychotics and strategies to avoid in order to prevent rebound psychosis, aggravation of side effects, or withdrawal symptoms.

Generally, it is preferable to (1) not rush the discontinuation of the first antipsychotic, (2) not allow gaps between two antipsychotic treatments, and (3) not start the second antipsychotic at full dose.

Switching from One Sedating Antipsychotic to Another

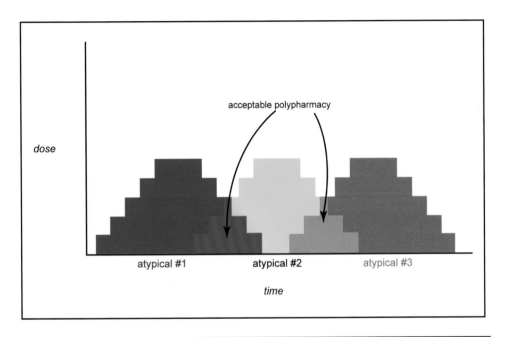

FIGURE 5.10. Cross-titration is usually advised when switching from one sedating antipsychotic to another. As the first antipsychotic is slowly tapered off, the second antipsychotic is slowly added on. This can be done over a few days or a few weeks.

Even though the patient will be simultaneously taking two medications for a short period of time, this is acceptable as it can decrease side effects and the risk of rebound symptoms, and it can hasten the successful transition to the second drug.

Getting Trapped in Cross-Titration

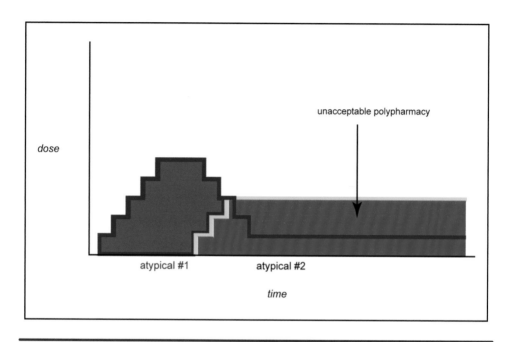

FIGURE 5.11. When initiating cross-titration, it is imperative to not forget to taper the first drug. Patients may improve in the middle of a cross-titration, but this should not be the reason to stop the process. An unfinished cross-titration will lead to polypharmacy where the patient takes two drugs indefinitely.

While polypharmacy is sometimes a necessity in hard-to-treat cases, an adequate monotherapy trial of a second drug should be the first option.

Use of Benzodiazepines to "Lead In" or "Top Up" Nonsedating Antipsychotics

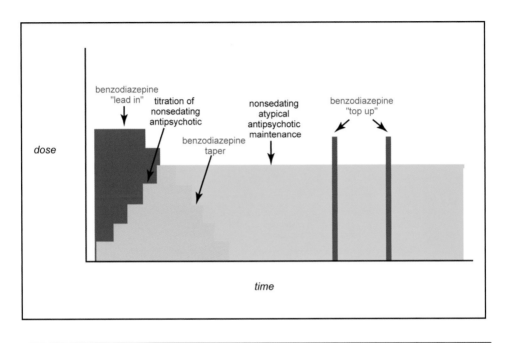

FIGURE 5.12. Benzodiazepines have been useful to either "lead in" or "top up" a nonsedating antipsychotic.

When patients are agitated, it may be beneficial to augment with a benzodiazepine just for a short time when the nonsedating antipsychotic is initiated. Thus the benzodiazepine is used as a "lead in" to the nonsedating anti-psychotic.

Once the nonsedating antipsychotic has been titrated to its full dose, then the benzodiazepine can be slowly tapered. Additionally, during the maintenance phase of the antipsychotic it can be helpful to use a benzodiazepine as a "top up" when needed by the patient.

Switching from a Sedating to a Nonsedating Antipsychotic

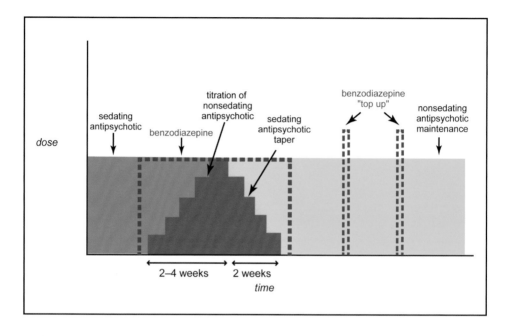

FIGURE 5.13. Switching from a sedating to a nonsedating antipsychotic can be problematic. One method for doing this is shown above. First a benzodiazepine is added, and then the nonsedating antipsychotic is titrated to its optimal therapeutic dose, while the sedating antipsychotic is still given at full dose. At this point the sedating antipsychotic is slowly tapered, while keeping the benzodiazepine present. When the patient is stable, the benzodiazepine can be tapered or stopped. Occasionally the benzodiazepine can be used to "top up" the patient and treat agitation or insomnia.

This switching strategy may be best for patients who are switching due to lack of adequate control of symptoms by their sedating antipsychotic. For those who are switching due to intolerability, the temporary polypharmacy of three agents may lead to side effects.

Switching from an SDA to a DPA:
Not Too Fast

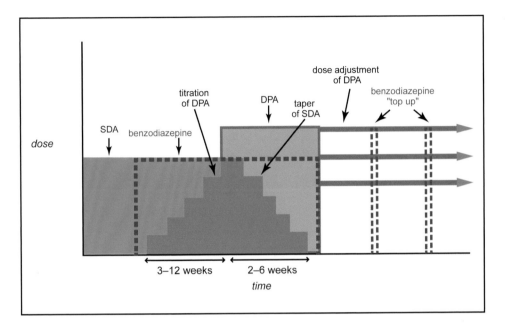

FIGURE 5.14. The emergence of psychosis, agitation, and insomnia can potentially burden the switch from a 5HT2A/D2 antagonist (SDA) to a D2 partial agonist (DPA). It may be best to initially add the second antipsychotic gradually while keeping the first one at full dose, and to keep both medications on board for a few weeks. It may also be beneficial to add a benzodiazepine short-term.

As soon as the patient is stable, the benzodiazepine can be tapered or stopped. Occasionally the benzodiazepine can be used to "top up" the patient and treat agitation or insomnia. When switching to a partial D2 agonist, it is important to give the receptors time to adjust their sensitivity, and thus the dose of the DPA may need to be adjusted in order to reach full therapeutic potential.

When Several Antipsychotic Monotherapies Fail

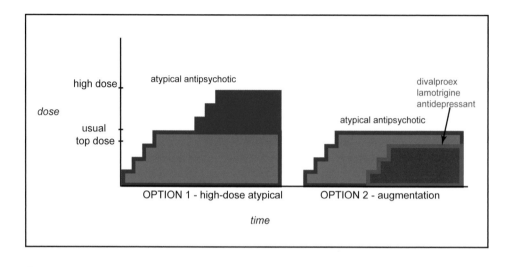

FIGURE 5.15. When a monotherapy with an atypical antipsychotic fails, the psychopharmacologist has few options.

Left: A high dose of the atypical antipsychotic can be used; however at high doses some side effects might appear that are normally not related to atypical antipsychotics.

Right: Augmentation with a mood stabilizer such as divalproex or lamotrigine or with an antidepressant could transform a previously ineffective atypical antipsychotic monotherapy into an efficacious drug cocktail.

When All Else Fails

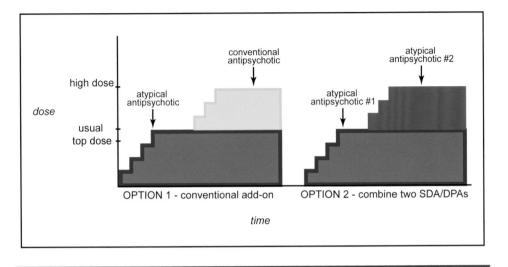

FIGURE 5.16. When pushing the dose of an atypical antipsychotic or augmenting it with other drugs still fails, it might be necessary to combine two antipsychotics. A conventional antipsychotic (left), or an atypical antipsychotic such as an SDA or DPA (right) can be added to the first atypical drug.

While antipsychotic polypharmacy is frequently practiced, it has not been well-studied and should only be used when every other approach has failed.

Stahl's Illustrated | Summary

- The underlying pathophysiology of schizophrenia remains to be fully elucidated.

- Dopamine, glutamate, and serotonin are three of the most important neurotransmitter systems involved in schizophrenia and in the mechanism of action of conventional and atypical antipsychotics.

- Each antipsychotic has a unique receptor profile, important in the alleviation of symptoms and induction of side effects.

- Atypical antipsychotics can have cardiometabolic risks, and thus patients need to be monitored when treatment is initiated.

- Today's psychopharmacologist has many choices when it comes to choosing an antipsychotic and can individualize treatment with the goals of maximizing treatment and minimizing side effects.

- It is necessary for psychopharmacologists to understand the art of switching between different antipsychotics, as patients will most likely have to try different medications in order to reach an optimal treatment plan.

5HT	serotonin
A	amygdala
ACh	acetylcholine
AChEI	acetylcholinesterase inhibitor
AMPA	alpha-amino-3-hydroxy-5-methyl-4-isoxazoleproprion-ic acid
BP	blood pressure
BF	basal forebrain
BMI	body mass index
BZ	benzodiazepine
C	cerebellum
CYP450	cytochrome P450 system
DA	dopamine
DKA	diabetic ketoacidosis
DLPFC	dorsolateral prefrontal cortex
DPA	dopamine 2 partial agonist
EPS	extrapyramidal side effects
GABA	gamma-aminobutyric acid
glu	glucose
GLU	glutamate
GlyT1	glycine transporter
H	hippocampus
HA	histamine
Hy	hypothalamus

Li	lithium
mGluR	metabotropic glutamate receptor
NA	nucleus accumbens
NE	norepinephrine
NMDA	N-methyl-*d*-aspartate
NRI	norepinephrine reuptake inhibitor
NT	brainstem neurotransmitter center
PA	partial agonist
PAM	positive allosteric modulator
PCP	phencyclidine
PFC	prefrontal cortex
S	striatum
SC	spinal cord
SDA	serotonin 2A and dopamine 2 antagonist
SPA	serotonin 1A partial agonist
SSRI	selective serotonin reuptake inhibitor
T	thalamus
TG	triglycerides
VMPFC	ventromedial prefrontal cortex
VTA	ventral tegmental area

☠	Life-threatening or Dangerous Side Effects	💊	Drug Interactions
⚪	Tips and Pearls	♥	Cardiac Impairment
🧍🧍	Children and Adolescents	🫘	Renal Impairment
🤰	Pregnancy	🫀	Hepatic Impairment

Suggested Readings

Abbatecola AM, Rizzo MR, Barbieri M, Grella R, Arciello A, Laieta MT et al. Post prandial plasma glucose excursions and cognitive functioning in aged type 2 diabetics. Neurology 2006;67(7):235–40.

Agid O, Mamo D, Ginovart N, Vitcu I, Wilson AA, Zipursky RB et al. Striatal vs. extrastriatal dopamine D2 receptors in antipsychotic response — a double-blind pet study in schizophrenia. Neuropsychopharmacology 2007;32:1209–15.

Alphs LD, Summerfelt A, Lann H, Muller RJ. The negative symptom assessment: a new instrument to assess negative symptoms of schizophrenia. Psychopharmacol Bull1989;25(2):159–63.

Artaloytia JF, Arango C, Lahti A, Sanz J, Pascual A, Cubero P et al. Negative signs and symptoms secondary to antipsychotics: a double-blind, randomized trial of a single dose of placebo, haloperidol, and risperidone in healthy volunteers. Am J Psychiatry 2006;163(3):488–93.

Atmaca M, Kuloglu M, Tezcan E, Ustundag B. Serum leptin and triglyceride levels in patients on treatment with atypical antipsychotics. J Clin Psychiatry 2003;64(5):598–604.

Bai YM, Lin CC, Chen JY, Lin CY, Su TP, Chou P. Association of initial antipsychotic response to clozapine and long-term weight gain. Am J Psychiatry 2006;163:1276–9.

Bardin L, Kleven MS, Barret-Grevoz C, Depoortere R, Newman-Tancredi A. Antipsychotic-like vs. cataleptogenic actions in mice of novel antipsychotics having D2 antagonist and 5-HT1A agonist properties. Neuropsychopharmacology 2006;31:1869–79.

Bennett S, Gronier B. Modulation of striatal dopamine release in vitro by agonists of the glycineB site of NMDA receptors: interaction with antipsychotics. Eur J Pharmacol 2005;527:52–9.

Bota RG, Sagduyu K, Munro JS. Factors associated with the prodromal progression of schizophrenia that influence the course of the illness. CNS Spectr 2005;10(12):937–42.

Cannon TD, Glahn DC, Kim J, Van Erp TGH, Karlsgodt K, Cohen MS et al. Dorsolateral prefrontal cortex activity during maintenance and manipulation of information in working memory in patients with schizophrenia. Arch Gen

Psychiatry 2005;62:1071–80.

Chiu CC, Chen KP, Liu HC, Lu ML. The early effect of olanzapine and risperidone on insulin secretion in atypical-naive schizophrenic patients. J Clin Psychopharmacol 2006;26(5):504–7.

Citrome L, Jaffe A, Levine J, Martello D. Incidence, prevalence and surveillance for diabetes in New York State psychiatric hospitals, 1997–2004. Psychiatr Serv 2006;57(8)1132–9.

Citrome L, Macher JP, Salazar DE, Mallikaarjun S, Boulton DW. Pharmacokinetics of aripiprazole and concomitant carbamazepine. J Clin Psychopharmacol 2007;27(3):279–83.

Citrome L. Iloperidone for schizophrenia: a review of the efficacy and safety profile for this newly commercialised second-generation antipsychotic. Int J Clin Pract 2009;63(8):1237–48.

Citrome L. Paliperidone palmitate—review of the efficacy, safety, and cost of a new second-generation depot antipsychotic medication. Int J Clin Pract 2009 Nov 3 [Epub ahead of print].

Citrome L. Asenapine for schizophrenia and bipolar disorder: a review of the efficacy and safety profile for this newly approved sublingually absorbed second-generation antipsychotic. Int J Clin Pract 2009;63(12):1762–84.

Correll CU, Manu P, Olshanskiy V, Napolitano B, Kane JM, Malhotra AK. Cardiometabolic risk of second-generation antipsychotic medications during first-time use in children and adolescents. JAMA 2009;302(16):1765–73.

Coyle JT, Tsai G. The NMDA receptor glycine modulatory site: a therapeutic target for improving cognition and reducing negative symptoms in schizophrenia. Psychopharmacology 2004;174:32–8.

Coyle JT, Tsai G, Goff D. Converging evidence of NMDA receptor hypofunction in the pathophysiology of schizophrenia. Ann N Y Acad Sci 2003;1003:318–27.

Coyle JT. Glutamate and schizophrenia: beyond the dopamine hypothesis. Cell Mol Neurobiol 2006;26(4–6):365–84.

De Bartolomeis A, Fiore G, Iasevoli F. Dopamine-glutamate interaction and antipsychotics mechanism of action: implication for new pharmacological strategies in psychosis. Curr Pharm Design 2005;11:3561–94.

DiForti M, Lappin JM, Murray RM. Risk factors for schizophrenia—all roads lead to dopamine. Eur Neuropsychopharmacol 2007;17:S101–7.

Emsley R, Rabinowitz J, Medori R. Time course for antipsychotic treatment response in first-episode schizophrenia. Am J Psychiatry 2006;163:743–5.

Essock SM, Covell NH, Davis SM, Stroup TS, Rosenheck RA, Lieberman JA. Effectiveness of switching antipsychotic medications. Am J Psychiatry 2006;163(12):2090–5.

Fenton WS, Chavez MR. Medication-induced weight gain and dyslipidemia in patients with schizophrenia. Am J Psychiatry 2006;163:1697–1704.

Glenthoj BY, Mackeprang T, Svarer C, Rasmussen H, Pinborg LH, Friberg L et al. Frontal dopamine D2/3 receptor binding in drug naive first-episode schizophrenia patients correlates with positive psychotic symptoms and gender. Biol Psychiatry 2006;60:621–9.

Green MF, Marder SR, Glynn SM, McGurk SR, Wirshing WC, Wirshing DA et al. The neurocognitive effects of low-dose haloperidol: a two-year comparison with risperidone. Biol Psychiatry 2002;51:972–8.

Hedlund PB, Sutcliffe JG. Functional, molecular and pharmacological advances in 5-HT7 receptor research. Trends Pharmacol Sci 2004;25(9):481–6.

Henderson DC, Cagliero E, Copeland PM, Louie PM, Borba CP, Fan X et al. Elevated hemoglobin A1c as a possible indicator of diabetes mellitus and diabetic ketoacidosis in schizophrenia patients receiving atypical antipsychotics. J Clin Psychiatry 2007;68:533–41.

Heresco-Levy U, Bar G, Levin R, Ermilov M, Ebstein RP, Javitt DC. High glycine levels are associated with prepulse inhibition deficits in chronic schizophrenia patients. Schizophr Res 2007;91(1–3):14–21.

Heresco-Levy U, Javitt DC, Ebstein R, Vass Ag, Lichtenbwerg P, Bar G et al. D-serine efficacy as add-on pharmacotherapy to risperidone and olanzapine for treatment-refractory schizophrenia. Biol Psychiatry 2005;57:577–85.

Houseknecht KL, Robertson AS, Zavadoski W, Gibbs EM, Johnson DE, Rollema H. Acute effects of atypical antipsychotics on whole-body insulin resistance in rats: implications for adverse metabolic effects. Neuropsychopharmacology 2007;32:289–97.

Hoyer D, Hannon JP, Martin GR. Molecular, pharmacological and functional diversity of 5-HT receptors. Pharmacol Biochem Behav 2002;71:533–54.

Ingelman-Sundberg M. Pharmacogenetics of cytochrome P450 and its applications in drug therapy: the past, present and future. Trends in Pharmacol Sci 2004;25(4):193–200.

Javitt DC. Is the glycine site half saturated or half unsaturated? Effects of glutamatergic drugs in schizophrenia patients. Curr Opin Psychiatry 2006;19:151–7.

Javitt DC, Balla A, Burch S, Suckow R, Xie S, Sershen H. Reversal of phencyclidine-induced dopaminergic dysregulation by N-methyl-d-aspartate receptor/glycine-site agonists. Neuropsychopharmacology 2004;(29):300–7.

Jindal RD, Keshavan S. Critical role of M3 muscarinic receptor in insulin secretion. J Clin Psychopharmacol 2006;26(5):449–50.

Johnson DE, Yamazaki H, Ward KM, Schmidt AW, Lebel WS, Treadway JL et al. Inhibitory effects of antipsychotics on carbachol-enhanced insulin secretion from perifused rat islets. Diabetes 2005;54:1552–8.

Jones PB, Barnes TRE, Davies L, Dunn G, Lloyd H, Hayhurst KP, Murray RM et al. Randomized controlled trial of the effect on quality of life of second- vs. first-generation antipsychotic drugs in schizophrenia. Arch Gen Psychiatry 2006;63:1079–87.

Kahn RS, Schulz SC, Palazov VD, Reyes EB, Brecher M, Svensson O et al. Efficacy and tolerability of once daily extended release quetiapine fumarate in acute schizophrenia: a randomized, double blind, placebo controlled study. J Clin Psychiatry 2007;68(6):832–42.

Kalkman HO, Feuerbach D, Lotscher E, Schoeffter P. Functional characterization of the novel antipsychotic iloperidone at human D2, D3, Alpha2c, 5-HT6 and 5-HT1A receptors. Life Sci 2003;73:1151–9.

Kapur S, Lecrubier Y. editors. Dopamine in the pathophysiology and treatment of schizophrenia. London, Martin Dunitz; 2003.

Kapur S. Psychosis as a state of aberrant salience: a framework linking biology, phenomenology, and pharmacology in schizophrenia. Am J Psychiatry 2003;160(1):13–23.

Keefe RS, Bilder RM, Davis SM, Harvey PD, Palmer BW, Gold JM et al. Neurocognitive effects of antipsychotic medications in patients with chronic schizophrenia in the CATIE trial. Arch Gen Psychiatry 2007;64:633–47.

Keefe RS, Bilder RM, Harvey PD, Davis SM, Palmer BW, Gold JM et al. Baseline neurocognitive deficits in the CATIE schizophrenia trial. Neuropsychopharmacology 2006;31:2033–46.

Keefe RS, Seidman LJ, Christensen BK, Harner RM, Sharma T, Sitskoorn MM et al. Long-term neurocognitive effects of olanzapine or low-dose haloperidol in first episode psychosis. Biol Psychiatry 2006;59:97–105.

Kern RS, Green MF, Cornblatt BA, Owen JR, McQuade RD, Carson WH et al. The neurocognitive effects of aripiprazole: an open label comparison with olanzapine. Psychopharmacology 2006;187:312–20.

Kessler RM, Ansari MS, Riccardi P, Li R, Jayathilake K, Dawant B et al. Occupancy of striatal and extrastriatal dopamine D2 receptors by clozapine and quetiapine. Neuropsychopharmacology 2006;31:1991–2001.

Kessler RM, Ansari MS, Riccardi P, Li R, Jyathilake K, Dawant B et al. Occupancy of striatal and extrastriatal dopamine D2/D3 receptors by olanzapine and haloperidol. Neuropsychopharmacology 2005;30:2283–9.

Lambert BL, Cunningham FE, Miller DR, Dalack GW, Hur K. Diabetes risk associated with use of olanzapine, quetiapine, and risperidone in Veterans Health Administration patients with schizophrenia. Am J Epidemiol 2006;164:672–81.

Lamberti JS, Olson D, Crilly JF, Olivares T, Williams GC, Tu X et al. Prevalence of the metabolic syndrome among patients receiving clozapine. Am J Psychiatry 2006;163:1273–6.

Lane HY, Chang YC, Liu YC, Chiu CC, Tsai GE. Sarcosine or D-Serine add-on treatment for acute exacerbation of schizophrenia. Arch Gen Psychiatry 2005;62:1196–1204.

Lane HY, Huang CL, Wu PL, Liu YC, Chang YC, Lin PY et al. Glycine Transporter 1 inhibitor, N-methylglycine (sarcosine), added to clozapine for the treatment of schizophrenia. Biol Psychiatry 2006;60:645–9.

Lawler CP, Prioleau C, Lewis MM, Mak C, Jiang D, Schetz JA et al. Interactions of the novel antipsychotic aripiprazole (OPC-14597) with dopamine and serotonin receptor su types. Neuropsychopharmacology 1999;20(6):612–27.

Lencz T, Smith CW, McLaughlin D, Auther A, Nakayama E, Hovey L et al. Generalized and specific neurocognitive deficits in prodromal schizophrenia. Biol Psychiatry 2006;59:863–71.

Leucht S, Busch R, Math D, Kissling W, Kane JM. Early prediction of antipsychotic nonresponse among patients with schizophrenia. J Clin Psychiatry 2007;68(3):352–60.

Lieberman JA, Stroup TS, McEvoy JP, Swartz MS, Rosenheck RA, Perkins DO, et al. Effectiveness of antipsychotic drugs in patients with chronic schizophernia. N Engl J Med 2005;353(12):1209-23.

Lieberman JA, Tollefson GD, Charles C, Zipursky R, Sharma T, Kahn RS et al. Antipsychotic drug effects on brain morphology in first episode psychosis. Arch Gen Psychiatry 2005;62:361–70.

Lindenmayer JP, Khan A, Iskander A, Abad MT, Parker B. A randomized controlled trial of olanzapine versus haloperidol in the treatment of primary negative symptoms and neurocognitive deficits in schizophrenia. J Clin Psychiatry 2007;68(3):368–79.

Lipkovich I, Citrome L, Perlis R, Deberdt W, Jouston JP, Ahl J et al. Early predictors of substantial weight gain in bipolar patients treated with olanzapine. J Clin Psychopharmocol 2006;26(3):316–20.

Lynch G, Gall CM. Ampakines and the threefold path to cognitive enhancement. Trends Neurosci 2006;29:10.

McCreary AD, Glennon JC, Ashby Jr R, Meltzer HY, Li Z, Reinders JH et al. SLV313 (1-(2,3 dihydro-benzo[1,4] dioxin-5-yl)-4-[5-(4-fluoro-phenyl)-pyridin-3-ylmethyl]-piperazine monohydrochloride): a novel dopamine D2 receptor antagonist and 5-HT1A receptor agonist potential antipsychotic drug. Neuropsychopharmacology 2007;32:78–94.

McEvoy JP, Lieberman JA, Sroup TS, Davis SM, Meltzer HY, Rosenheck RA et al. Effectiveness of clozapine versus olanzapine, quetiapine, and risperidone in patients with chronic schizophrenia who did not respond to prior atypical antipsychotic treatment. Am J Psychiatry 2006;163:600–10.

McGlashan TH, Zipursky RB, Perkins D, Addington J, Miller T, Woods SW et al. Randomized, double-blind trial of olanzapine versus placebo in patients prodromally symptomatic for psychosis. Am J Psychiatry 2006;163:790–9.

McLaughlin T, Abbasi F, Cheal K, Chu J, Lamendola C, Reaven G. Use of metabolic markers to identify overweight individuals who are insulin resistant. Ann Intern Med 2003;139:802–9.

Meyer JM, Loebel AD, Schweizer E. Lurasidone: a new drug in development for schizophrenia. Expert Opin Investig Drugs 2009;18(11):1715–26.

Millan MJ. N-Methyl-d-aspartate receptors as a target for improved antipsychotic agents: novel insights and clinical perspectives. Psychopharmacology 2005;179:30–53.

Mizrahi R, Rusjan P, Agid O, Graff A, Mamo DC, Zipursky RB et al. Adverse subjective experience with antipsychotics and its relationship to striatal and extrastriatal D2 receptors: a PET study in schizophrenia. Am J Psychiatry 2007;164:630–7.

Murphy BP, Chung YC, Park TW, McGorry PD. Pharmacological treatment of primary negative symptoms in schizophrenia: a systematic review. Schizophr Res 2006;88:5–25.

Nakamura M, Ogasa M, Guarino J, Phillips D, Severs J, Cucchiaro J et al. Lurasidone in the treatment of acute schizophrenia: a double-blind, placebo-controlled trial. J Clin Psychiatry 2009;70(6):829–36.

Natesan S, Reckless GE, Barlow KBL, Nobrega JN, Kapur S. Evaluation of N-desmethylclozapine as a potential antipsychotic—preclinical studies. Neuropsychopharmacology 2007;32:1540–9.

Natesan S, Reckless GE, Nobrega JN, Fletcher PJ, Kapur S. Dissociation between in vivo occupancy and functional antagonism of dopamine D2 receptors: comparing aripiprazole to other antipsychotics in animal models. Neuropsychopharmacology 2006;31:1854–63.

Newman-Tancredi A, Assie MB, Leduc N, Ormiere AM, Danty N, Cosi C. Novel antipsychotics activate recombinant human and native rat serotonin 5-HT1A receptors: affinity, efficacy, and potential implications for treatment of schizophrenia. Int J Neuropsychopharmacol 2005;8:341–56.

Olfson M, Blanco C, Liu L, Moreno C, Laje G. National trends in the outpatient treatment of children and adolescents with antipsychotic drugs. Arch Gen Psychiatry 2006;63:679–85.

Olfson M, Marcus SC, Corey-Lisle P, Tuomari AV, Hines P, L'Italien GJ. Hyperlipidemia following treatment with antipsychotic medications. Am J Psychiatry 2006;163:1821–5.

Olincy A, Harris JG, Johnson LL, Pender V, Kongs S, Allensworth D et al. Proof-of-concept trial of an alpha 7 nicotinic agonist in schizophrenia. Arch Gen Psychiatry 2006;63:630–8.

Osborn DPJ, Levy G, Nazareth I, Petersen I, Islam A, King MB. Relative risk of cardiovascular and cancer mortality in people with severe mental illness from the United Kingdom's general practice research database. Arch Gen Psychiatry 2007;64:242–9.

Pierre JM, Peloian JH, Wirshing DA, Wirshing WC, Marder SR. A randomized, double-blind, placebo-controlled trial of modafinil for negative symptoms in schizophrenia. J Clin Psychiatry 2007;68(5):705–10.

Polsky D, Doshi JA, Bauer MS, Glick HA. Clinical trial-based cost effectiveness analyses of antipsychotic use. Am J Psychiatry 2006;163(12):2047–56.

Reaven G. The metabolic syndrome or the insulin resistance syndrome: different names, different concepts, and different goals. Endocrinol Metab Clin North Am 2004;33:283–303.

Reist C, Mintz J, Albers LJ, Jamas MM, Szabo S, Ozdemir V. Second-generation antipsychotic exposure and metabolic-related disorders in patients with schizophrenia. J Clin Psychopharmacol 2007;27:46–51.

Remington G, Mamo D, Labelle A, Reiss J, Shammi C, Mannaert E et al. A PET study evaluating dopamineD2 receptor occupancy for long-acting injectable risperidone. Am J Psychiatry 2006;163(3):396–401.

Reyes M, Buitelaar J, Toren P, Augustyns I, Eerdekens M. A randomized, double-blind, placebo-controlled study of risperidone maintenance treatment in children and adolescents with disruptive behavior disorders. Am J Psychiatry 2006;163:402–10.

Reynolds GP, Yao Z, Zhang XB, Sun J, Zhang ZJ. Pharmacogenetics of treatment in first-episode schizophrenia: D3 and 5-HT2C receptor polymorphisms separately associate with positive and negative symptom response. Eur Neuropsychopharmacol 2004;15:143–51.

Rosenheck RA, Leslie DL, Sindelar J, Miller EA, Lin H, Stroup TS et al. Cost-effectiveness of second generation antipsychotics and perphenazine in a randomized trial of treatment for chronic schizophrenia. Am J Psychiatry 2006;163(12):2080–9.

Sarter M. Preclinical research into cognition enhancers. Trends Pharmacol Sci 2006;27:11.

Sepehry AA, Potvin S, Elie R, Stip E. Selective serotonin reuptake inhibitor (SSRI) add-on therapy for the negative symptoms of schizophrenia: a meta-analysis. J Clin Psychiatry 2007;68(4):604–10.

Shayegan DK, Stahl SM. Emotion processing, the amygdala, and outcome in schizophrenia. Prog Neuropsychopharmacol Biol Psychiatry 2005;29:840–5.

Simonson GD, Kendall DM. Diagnosis of insulin resistance and associated syndromes: the spectrum from the metabolic syndrome to type 2 diabetes mellitus. Coron Artery Dis 2005;16:465–72.

Smid P, Coolen HKAC, Keizer HG, van Hes R, de Moes JP, den Hartog AP et al. Synthesis, structure-activity relationships, and biological properties of 1-heteroaryl-4-[Ω-(1H-indol-3-yl) alkyl]piperazines, novel potential antipsychotics combining potent dopamine D2 receptor antagonism with potent serotonin reuptake inhibition. J Med Chem 2005;48:6855–69.

Spurling RD, Lamberti JS, Olsen D, Tu X, Tang W. Changes in metabolic parameters with switching to aripiprazole from another second-generation antipsychotic: a retrospective chart review. J Clin Psychiatry 2007;68(3):406–9.

Stahl SM. Prophylactic antipsychotics: do they keep you from catching schizophrenia? J Clin Psychiatry 2004;65(11):1445–6.

Stahl SM. Stahl's Essential Psychopharmacology, 3rd Edition, Cambridge University Press, N.Y., 2008.

Stahl SM. Stahl's Essential Psychopharmacology: Prescriber's Guide, 2nd Edition, Cambridge University Press, N.Y., 2006.

Stroup TS, Lieberman JA, McEvoy JP, Swartz MS, Davis SM, Capuano GA et al. Effectiveness of olanzapine, quetiapine, and risperidone in patients with chronic schizophrenia after discontinuing perphenazine: a CATIE study. Am J Psychiatry 2007;164:415–27.

Takahashi H, Higuchi M, Suhara T. The role of extrastriatal dopamine D2 receptors in schizophrenia. Biol Psychiatry 2006;59:919–28.

Talkowski ME, Mansour H, Chowdari KV, Wood J, Butler A, Varma PG et al. Novel, replicated associations between dopamine D3 receptor gene polymorphisms and schizophrenia in two independent samples. Biol Psychiatry 2006;60:570–7.

Tarazi FI, Baldessarini RJ, Kula NS, Zhang K. Long-term effects of olanzapine, risperidone, and quetiapine on ionotropic glutamate receptor types: implications for antipsychotic drug treatment. J Pharmacol Exp Ther 2003;306(3):1145–51.

Tenback DE, van Harten PN, Sloof CJ, van Os J. Evidence that early extrapyramidal symptoms predict later tardive dyskinesia: a prospective analysis of 10,000 patients in the European schizophrenia outpatient health outcomes (SOHO) study. Am J Psychiatry 2006;163:1438–40.

Tran-Johnson TK, Sack DA, Marcus RN, Auby P, McQuade RD, Oren DA. Efficacy and safety of intramuscular aripiprazole in patients with acute agitation: a randomized, double-blind, placebo-controlled trial. J Clin Psychiatry 2007;68(1):111–9.

Tsai G, Lane HY, Chong MY, Lange N. Glycine transporter 1 inhibitor, N-methylglycine (sarcosine), added to antipsychotics for the treatment of schizophrenia. Biol Psychiatry 2004;55:452–6.

Vestri HS, Maianu L, Moellering DR, Garvey WT. Atypical antipsychotic drugs directly impair insulin action in adipocytes: effects on glucose transport, lipogenesis, and antilipolysis. Neuropsychopharmacology 2007;32:765–72.

Vidalis AA. Psychopharmacology issues in pregnancy and lactation. Thessasloniki, Greece, Contemporary Editions; 2006.

Weissman EM, Zhu CW, Schooler NR, Goetz RR, Essock SM. Lipid monitoring in patients with schizophrenia prescribed second generation antipsychotics. J Clin Psychiatry 2006;67(9):1323–6.

Wezenberg E, Verkes RJ, Ruigt GSF, Hulstijn W, Sabbe BGC. Acute effects of the ampakine farampator on memory and information processing in healthy elderly volunteers. Neuropsychopharmacology 2007;32:1272–83.

Yaeger D, Smith HG, Altshuler LL. Atypical antipsychotics in the treatment of schizophrenia during pregnancy and the postpartum. Am J Psychiatry 2006;163(12):2064–70.

Zhang M, Ballard ME, Kohlhaas KL, Browmna KE, Jongen-Relo AL, Unger LV et al. Effect of dopamine D3 antagonists on PPI in DBA/2J mice or PPI deficit induced by neonatal ventral hippocampal lesions in rats. Neuropsychopharmacology 2006;31:1382–92.